PURE
& SIMPLE

DELICIOUS RECIPES FOR
ADDITIVE-FREE COOKING

OTHER BOOKS BY MARIAN BURROS
(WITH LOIS LEVINE)

ELEGANT BUT EASY

SECOND HELPINGS

FREEZE WITH EASE

COME FOR COCKTAILS, STAY FOR SUPPER

THE SUMMERTIME COOKBOOK

PURE & SIMPLE

DELICIOUS RECIPES FOR ADDITIVE-FREE COOKING

An Elegant & Easy Cookbook
with Up-To-Date Advice on
Avoiding Ingredients that Contain
Chemicals & Preservatives

By MARIAN BURROS

WILLIAM MORROW AND COMPANY, INC.
NEW YORK   1978

Library of Congress Cataloging in Publication Data

Burros, Marian Fox.
   Pure & simple.

   Includes index.
   1. Cookery (Natural foods) I. Title.
TX741.B87   641.5   77-28578
ISBN 0-688-03285-0

BOOK DESIGN   CARL WEISS

Printed in the United States of America.

5   6   7   8   9   10

ACKNOWLEDGMENTS

I F PEOPLE FIND *Pure & Simple* useful, it will be thanks to the efforts of a lot of people. Credit for the accuracy and clarity of the information, and the workability of the recipes, is shared by many, some of whom prefer anonymity!

Among those willing to be counted, I want to especially thank my husband, Donald. In addition to being the best chopper and slicer any cook can have, he is the taster par excellence. His approval or disapproval of a newly created recipe determined whether or not anyone else ever got to taste it.

My daughter, Ann, who helped me prove an important point about the inconvenience of convenience foods, as recounted elsewhere in the book, is also an excellent critic of taste.

My son, Michael, tested several recipes, contributed a few new ones and raised my consciousness about vegetarian dishes.

Over the years Shang Patterson has tested hundreds of recipes for me in my work as a newspaper food editor. She did yeoman's service on the book, especially in the convenience-food section.

My dear friend Sherley Koteen graciously agreed to read the manuscript to make sure it was intelligible to lay persons.

Joan Dye Gussow, chairman of the program in nutrition education at Columbia University Teachers College, read the first chapter as a nutrition educator and professional editor. Her help was invaluable. It is because of such a good friend and colleague that I haven't put my foot in my mouth.

If the book works, my friends and family deserve a lot of the credit; if it doesn't, blame me.

M.F.B.

Bethesda, Maryland
September, 1977

CONTENTS

INTRODUCTION

Sugar, hydrogenated coconut and soybean oils, propylene glycol, mono-stearate (emulsifier for uniform blending of oils), corn syrup solids, sodium caseinate (a protein), whey solids, sodium silico aluminate (prevents caking), hydroxylated soybean lecithin and acetylated mono-glycerides (emulsifiers), artificial flavor and color, BHA (a preservative).

THAT LIST OF UNRECOGNIZABLE, UNPRONOUNCEABLE INGREDIENTS produces fake whipped cream, found frequently on top of a chocolate mousse, spread over pumpkin pie or as a garnish for an ice cream parfait. You can recognize the product by its unreal whiteness and oily aftertaste.

Have you ever wondered how much this ersatz cream costs compared to genuine heavy whipping cream?

Have you ever wondered what all those ingredients might be?

In the late Fifties and early Sixties I never gave such questions a thought. Like the vast majority of other Americans I couldn't wait to try the newest convenience product. Advertising had conned me into believing, just as it had almost everyone else, that what came out of the laboratories of the big food companies tasted better, was cheaper than anything I could make at home and would save me hours of drudgery in the kitchen.

But I was lucky. I was exposed to some of the finest cooking in the world through travel to France and Italy. And by one of those strange twists of fate, just as I was beginning to question the taste of the highly processed foods, I began to get little hints that some of the things being put into them might not be safe either. Eventually it dawned on me that in addition to a lack of taste and the questions of safety, I was paying too much for these foods which were also short on nutrition.

So over the years I have moved away from highly processed or so-called convenience foods. This chapter, I hope, explains why.

PROCESSED FOOD: WHAT IT MEANS

By the time any food arrives at the supermarket it has been processed in some way, but there are degrees, from the simplest defuzzing of peaches and the more complex cutting up of a steer into family-size portions, to the kind of processing that produces fake whipped cream.

Sometimes the processing yields products that imitate natural foods—albeit poorly—with combinations of chemicals that never quite make it on the taste scale and definitely don't make it when it comes to providing various micronutrients and trace minerals found in real foods.

Frequently technology destroys the integrity of the natural product by removing most of the nutrients; it often adulterates the raw material by adding a variety of additives. Some additives provide longer shelf life or keep ingredients from separating. Others offer bright new colors, change the flavor or texture. Still others replace the expensive valuable nutrients with cheap ones to increase profitability. Almost without exception, these highly processed foods are far more costly than what is made at home from scratch.

After all, when you prepare food at home, no one is paying you factory labor rates to add a pat of butter to a pot of peas or put the peas-in-butter-sauce into one of those plastic pouches, which also take a tremendous amount of fossil fuel energy to produce. This makes the peas-in-butter-sauce in the boil-in-the-bag pouch in the coated-paper carton cost 20 cents more than the ingredients are actually worth. But the greatest profitability for the food manufacturer is in the highly processed foods, and they often turn out to be those with the least nutritional value. They certainly are the ones with the most food additives.

PROCESSED FOODS: THE COST FACTOR

The purchase of most highly processed foods such as sauce mixes, Hamburger Helper, orange juice substitutes and vegetable dishes with sauce usually does mean overpayment. We have been conned by advertising into believing that we not only don't want to take the time to make these seemingly complicated dishes with dozens of unpronounceable ingredients, but we really aren't capable. Besides, don't cake mixes taste just as good, even better, than homemade cakes? Aren't soups made from a chemical feast just as good as Grandma's? (Only if Grandma was a food technologist in a white lab coat.) How about those seasonings for ground beef that are supposed to put from-scratch creations to shame in half the time?,

The answer is a resounding "No!" But if we are unable to make cakes from scratch, part of the problem may be that no one has ever taught us. Many home-economics classes in school show students only how to open a box, pour the contents into a bowl, and add an egg and some water.

Of course, someone at home should be doing the teaching, and probably anyone who has gotten this far in the book isn't letting his or her children grow up ignorant of the fact that warm mixtures must be added slowly to uncooked eggs; that flour can't be added to liquid without making a paste first; that real food tastes better than fake.

Another sad and ironic point is that in most cases convenience foods aren't that convenient. Hamburger Helper is a wonderful example. So are salad-dressing mixes, pancake mixes, flavored rice—the list is endless.

We did a time-and-motion study with Hamburger Helper once, just for fun. The anchorman on the evening news at WRC-TV, NBC's Washington station where I work, pooh-poohed a piece I did that explained why it is cheaper and quicker and better to make Hamburger Helper from scratch. I challenged him to a Hamburger Helper cookoff with my thirteen-year-old daughter.

I taught her the basic elements that give flavor to one of the Hamburger Helper varieties, minus all the unnecessary chemicals. With or without the box, you still have to supply the meat and brown it and cook the noodles. My daughter, Ann, cooked her from-scratch version in under five minutes; the anchorman, Jim Vance, took over eight. He was convinced, especially after he tasted hers and liked the flavor better! Moreover, the cost factor put a double whammy on the whole game. At the time a box of Hamburger Helper cost 69 cents, but with noodles from a box, a can of tomato sauce and the seasonings, the from-scratch version cost only 45 cents.

PROCESSED FOODS: THE SAFETY FACTOR

With the banning of certain additives over the last several years you must have wondered about the safety of those still in the food.

If you have, you probably dismissed such questions as unimportant, because, after all, the store wouldn't sell you anything that wasn't safe to eat. Right?

Wrong!

You were right to wonder but wrong to assume that everything added to food is safe and throughly tested.

Perhaps you react as the First Lady, Rosalynn Carter, told me she did when she used to do her own grocery shopping. In October, 1976, Mrs. Carter said she was concerned about the additives put in food. "It bothers me a little. I do try to read ingredients but I haven't had time to become really concerned, because I do so little cooking now and I use so few of those things.

"I know how distressed I get in the grocery store [when something isn't labeled]. You have to know what you're eating."

The Food and Drug Administration, which is supposed to oversee the safety of what may be put into food, has an extremely difficult job. There are several reasons for this. The nature of the federal bureaucracy is to leave things as they are, not to rock the boat. In addition, the pressures brought by special-interest groups such as the food industry, which want to conduct business with as little government intervention as possible, are extremely powerful. And the countervailing force—you and me, the consumer—is pitifully small and weak in comparison.

It doesn't help that many of the important officials in the FDA have worked for the food industry which they are supposed to be regulating, or plan to join the industry when they leave the FDA. Such regulators do not regulate with the kind of impartiality and steely-eyed objectivity needed. Though the FDA Commissioner appointed by President Carter, Dr. Donald Kennedy, has no such ties and has earned high marks from consumer advocates for some of his actions, there is a long way to go. So many additives in use have never been tested properly. And the process of testing them is lengthy.

Thus the safety of food additives is not what it should be. Every year brings the banning or petition for banning of another chemical that has been added to food for decades. In 1976 Red Number 2 and Red Number 4 food colors were finally banished from foods. That same year the FDA was petitioned to ban all of the other coal-tar-based dyes along with sodium nitrite, found in most processed meats. The attempt by the FDA to ban saccharin made headlines in March, 1977. And the governmental group studying food additives already in use put out a report that said there might be problems with BHT, an additive used to prevent oils from turning rancid. BHT has been removed from the GRAS (Generally Recognized As Safe) list and placed in an interim category which permits continued use while further testing is conducted. In the meantime a petition to ban BHT has been presented to the FDA. The same government-appointed group studying additives also said that hydrolized vegetable protein (HVP) should be taken out of baby food. Generally, the public is not even aware that questions of safety have arisen about a food additive until something drastic, such as a ban, is imminent.

In 1976 it became abundantly clear that some tests of safety submitted to the FDA by a manufacturer wishing to market a new additive had been rigged. Companies have juggled statistical results to prove safety; the records kept on test animals have been sloppy or, worse, altered. (The FDA is investigating some of these companies and tests now.) So it's a little difficult to have faith in the safety of the food supply, particularly the safety of processed foods.

The food industry argues that there are many hazardous substances occurring *naturally* in foods. And they are right. There are many hazardous substances which make their way into food, not just from pesticides, fungicides and herbicides, but from the water, air and earth itself: DDT, PBB's, PCB's end up in food and then in us—unintentionally, of course. This fact leads some people to conclude that if an additive is not absolutely safe, what difference does it make? Of course! But why make matters worse? As Dr. Jean Mayer, formerly professor of nutrition at Harvard University and now president of Tufts University, wrote in the introduction to *Eater's Digest: A Consumer's Factbook of Food Additives*, "any added chemical of necessity increases the risk, albeit by a small amount." If you keep adding up these small amounts, pretty soon the amount isn't so small anymore. And there is no way to know how much of such potentially dangerous substances are needed to cause birth defects or cancer.

Cancer experts say there is no known level at which a carcinogen (cancer-causing agent) can be considered safe. One then has to decide whether or not it is worth taking the risk. Do the benefits of eating bacon or ham cured with sodium nitrite, or beef liver contaminated with traces of diethylstilbestrol (DES), outweigh the risks? What about saccharin? It is considered a weak carcinogen, but that does not mean that you would have to drink eight hundred bottles of diet soda a day to get cancer, as the diet industry would have you believe. It simply means that it takes more of a weak carcinogen than of a strong one to cause cancer; it takes longer for tumors to develop and fewer people in the population will be stricken.

Is using saccharin worth the risk? Maybe, if you are diabetic, though many doctors who specialize in the treatment of diabetes say it is not essential, that desire for sweet things should be satisfied with naturally sweet foods such as fruits.

Most saccharin, however, is not used by diabetics. It is used by soda-pop drinkers, especially teen-agers and young adults. Unfortunately, this puts those believed to be at greatest risk—unborn children—at the mercy of what the mother-to-be has been drinking. In the famous Canadian rat study on which the proposed saccharin ban is based, the greatest number of malignant tumors occurred in the animals whose mothers had been fed saccharin while they were carrying the fetuses.

Do the benefits—so far undetermined—outweigh the risks? Only if you are in the business of selling diet sodas, it seems to me!

Mrs. Carter told me in an interview with her before she became First Lady that her gut reaction to potential hazards in the food supply is "remove it. Find out if it is safe and then put it back on the market. We ought not wait until after it's tested," she said. "I don't think we should suffer until we find out."

The benefits of food additives are often benefits for food manufacturers. For example, by adding BHT to a box of its product, a cereal company can give it a shelf life of two years. But who keeps cereal at home for two years?

Certainly the artificial red coloring and artificial strawberry flavoring in most strawberry ice cream does nothing for the consumer. But by adding red coloring and artificial flavor the producer doesn't have to put in very many strawberries, if any! Sure, this is cheaper than naturally colored and flavored ice cream; but when you compare the taste and quality, no matter how cheap the artificial product is, it isn't worth the price. You know how true that is if you have ever left cheap ice cream on the drainboard overnight and returned the next morning to find a gummy mass where there had once been a great big half-gallon. What happened? In addition to the synthetic ingredients in the cheap ice cream, so much air has been beaten into it that when it melts, there's very little real substance left.

Since artificial colors are under a deep cloud of suspicion as potentially dangerous and certainly insufficiently tested, why eat them? Because through conditioning we have come to expect our food to look a certain way.

Ruth Winter, author of *A Consumer's Dictionary of Food Additives*, thinks she knows what happened:

> We want enhanced food because all of our lives we have been subjected to beautiful pictures of foods in our magazines and on television. We have come to expect an advertiser's concept of perfection in color and texture, even though Mother Nature may not turn out all her products that way. As a result the skin of the oranges we eat are dyed bright orange to match our mental image of an ideal orange.

A Swedish journalist, visiting here several summers ago, brought the point home very quickly. She made short shrift of the introductory pleasantries when we met. What she really wanted to know was why our cheeses were such a funny color. In Sweden, she said, they didn't have artificially colored cheeses, and orange seemed a peculiar shade! Orange Cheddar cheese doesn't taste any different from natural creamy-colored Cheddar, but some people think orange cheese means expensive aged cheese. It doesn't. Bright-orange Cheddar cheese versus naturally colored cheese appears to be a matter of economic deception. This is certainly the case with the orange color in orange breakfast drinks. Such drinks are colored orange to make them look like orange juice. They are flavored to make them taste a little like orange juice and even have a few of the nutrients found in the real thing. But they don't contain the trace nutrients found in real oranges which are essential to health. And clearly they don't taste like the real thing!

LABEL LANGUAGE: WHAT IT MEANS

How many times have you looked at a label on a can or box and seen words such as "enriched" or "fortified" or even "antioxidant" and wondered exactly what those terms meant? Probably many times! I've tried here to provide a working knowledge of a few of the more commonly used terms.

Enrichment

Are all the chemical additives risky? Certainly the ones which have been singled out here are: sodium nitrite, saccharin, DES, artificial colors and BHT. But some additives actually do relatively good things. In certain foods some, but not all, of the vitamins and minerals which had been stripped away in the processing are re-added. In this case additives are good, or at least harmless. The process of re-adding vitamins and minerals is called *enrichment* and is used for such foods as breads, white rice, and cereals.

Fortification

Fortification, or adding nutrients to foods that didn't have them even before processing, is another relatively beneficial process. However, no amount of fortifying with a few nutrients is going to turn junk food into good food.

Those dreadful "fortified" cupcakes, sometimes served as part of the school-breakfast program in some places, are a perfect example. (The Department of Agriculture, under Secretary Bob Bergland, proposed removing them from the program in 1977.) Even if such a cupcake had 100 percent of the Recommended Daily Allowance of the eight vitamins and minerals used in nutrition labeling, it would still be totally unsuitable for breakfast, as are breakfast bars and other candies, cookies and fortified sweets. They contain too much sugar, too much fat and, in certain cases, undesirable additives such as artificial color.

Vitamins and minerals, of course, are good guys, and their addition to food is not all bad. The iron used to fortify bread and the iodine added to salt are examples of beneficial fortification. But for the most part it's better to obtain nutrients directly from their natural source.

Flavor Enhancers

Flavor enhancers are used to bring out the flavor in foods but, in fact, reduce the amount of natural (and more expensive) ingredients needed in food. The ubiquitous monosodium glutamate (MSG) is such a product. It's hard to find any prepared products for entrees and side dishes without it.

Besides the fact that MSG makes manufactured chicken soup seem as if it contains a lot of chicken when it may contain very little or none, MSG has an unpleasant, allergic effect on many, many people. MSG causes what is known as the Chinese Restaurant Syndrome because the reaction was discovered by a doctor after he ate Chinese food. Symptoms include tightness in the neck, base of the skull, head and chest, as well as dizziness. The reaction passes within a few hours, fortunately.

Thickening Agents and Stabilizers

Thickening agents and stabilizers are needed when inferior ingredients or poor manufacturing practices are used which might result in a watery or lumpy product. Thickening agents, such as modified food starch, are used in cheap yogurt to give it the same consistency as properly made yogurt.

Preservatives and Antioxidants

Preservatives and antioxidants prevent spoilage, but often they are not necessary except to give the product an extremely long shelf life or to cover up poor manufacturing practices.

The best-known preservatives are sodium nitrite and sodium nitrate (nitrates convert to nitrites). Sodium nitrite is used in almost all processed meats; sodium nitrate in a few. In the stomachs of test animals nitrites combine with substances called amines, found in other foods, drugs and tobacco smoke, to form potent carcinogens called nitrosamines. In bacon, however, nitrosamines are formed when the product is fried.

Sodium nitrite is also a flavor enhancer and a coloring agent. (It makes processed meats pink.) It also is used to prevent the formation of the botulism toxins, which can be fatal. However, there are other methods to ensure the safety of processed meats. The old-fashioned long curing of bacon and ham produces not only the same result, but provides what some consider a superior taste. To preserve other processed meats without nitrites, such as bologna, salami, liverwurst, hot dogs, turkey ham, chicken hot dogs, freezing is safe and effective.

There are alternatives to nitrites, but the large manufacturers aren't listening. In September, 1977, the U. S. Department of Agriculture and the FDA told manufacturers of processed meats that they would have to prove specifically that nitrosamines did not form in their products before they hit the stomach and that their use of sodium nitrite was not only essential but safe. The saga of sodium nitrite has been unfolding for many years, but with increased intensity since 1973. A resolution to the problem may be a long way off.

Probably less hazardous but totally unnecessary are the antioxidants BHA (butylated hydroxyanisole) and its close relative BHT (butylated hydroxymethylphenol). Some potato-chip manufacturers don't find it necessary to use either chemical, so obviously they aren't essential, but most potato, corn and tortilla chips contain BHA and/or BHT. Some salad oils and shortening contain one or both chemicals; some don't. This is true for cereals, too. The so-called natural cereals use neither chemical yet they last on the grocers' shelves for nine months or longer. You must read the label to find out where these antioxidants are.

Artificial Colors

Artificial colors, which are purely cosmetic, may be on their way out over the next ten years or so. Either the coal-tar-based dyes have been poorly tested or tests have shown potential hazards. These artificial colors also may cause hyperactivity in some children.

Food colorings can be listed simply as "artificial color" or "FD&C certified coloring," which refers to an FDA food, drug and cosmetic regulation. There is no way to know what such colors are.

Yellow Number 5, also called tartrazine, is a special case because many people are allergic to it. The FDA has proposed that foods containing Yellow Number 5 indicate the presence of the color on the label.

Since artificial colors are potentially hazardous and unnecessary, why eat anything in which they are found? There has been a move toward the use of "natural" food colorings recently, primarily because one by one, artificial colors are being banned. When a label reads "natural color," the coloring agent might be something harmless such as paprika, turmeric or grape skins. But it does not mean the color of the product is its natural color.

A former Commissioner of the FDA, Dr. Alexander Schmidt, said:

> When we take luxury versus necessity into consideration, we begin to move solidly into the area of foods. Certain substances with which we deal, cosmetics for example . . . are not essential to support life, and

therefore should present no risk whatsoever. I have yet to see a really convincing, comprehensive, and quantitative analysis of the benefits of food additives. . . . Some must be described as cosmetic. And we've already established that cosmetics should be without risk.

Artificial Flavors

No matter the flavor, food technologists would have you believe that it is impossible to tell the difference between natural and artificial flavors. But if you have a fairly well developed palate, you can. The artificial flavor often leaves a strange aftertaste; sometimes it doesn't have any recognizable taste at all.

Have you ever tasted an artificially flavored product blindfolded? It's often impossible to tell what the flavor is without a clue from the name or picture. With sweets the overriding taste is usually not flavor, but sweetness.

Meat Analogs

Imitation meat is made of processed soy protein, which has an appearance, texture and nutritive value something like meat. It is used extensively in prepared beef stews, ground-meat products such as spaghetti sauces, and even prepared fish products. It is very cheap and is listed on the label as textured vegetable protein (TVP), textured soy protein or isolated soy protein. But if you want a substitute for meat, you're better off with complementary proteins such as beans and rice, or milk products, even eggs.

LABEL READING: HOW TO DO IT; PACKAGING: WHAT TO LOOK FOR

And *you* can do something about all the other additives, too. If you don't like being ripped off, if you care about how things taste, if you worry about polluting your body with untested or poorly tested substances, you can move away from highly processed foods. You have to learn how to read labels and you have to be selective about raw ingredients.

After January 1, 1978, if all went according to government plan, it should have become a bit easier to find out what is in most processed foods. As of that date, only the following foods still were not required to list all ingredients: cocoa products, macaroni and noodle products, milk and cream, natural cheeses (as opposed to processed cheeses, which are required to list ingredients), food flavorings, mayonnaise and salad dressings, some canned fruits, fruit juices and vegetables, bread, butter and ice cream. By July 1, 1979, ice cream is supposed to carry ingredient labeling. Some food products, such as mayonnaise and salad dressing, appear to be listing all ingredients now, but that is not necessarily the case.

Ingredients are listed in order of predominance, so if water is the first ingredient there is more water in the product than anything else.

The use of additives in unprocessed foods is a little trickier. There are some fruits and vegetables which don't have to indicate the presence of artificial color: Florida oranges, which are dyed during certain months (but not those from California or Arizona); red potatoes; some sweet potatoes.

Much of the produce in the supermarkets is waxed: apples, tomatoes, cucumbers, potatoes, cantaloupes, oranges, bell peppers, lemons, pears, grapefruits, plums, yams. The box in the back room may indicate the presence of wax, but nothing at the point of sale does. You must either peel these fruits and vegetables or wash them thoroughly. Some people go so far as to use Ivory soap to wash them.

Then, of course, there are the *hidden* additives. Keep in mind that many of the chemical residues which are polluting our world end up in the fat of animals. This and the other unhealthful aspects of eating too much fat are excellent reasons for sticking with lean meats and cutting away excess fat.

Most processed meats are also loaded with fat, so they are a very expensive source of protein. You'd have to eat ten slices of bacon or six slices of bologna to get the same amount of protein found in one three-ounce hamburger. Three ounces of hamburger cost about 22 cents; ten slices of bacon cost $1.15; six slices of bologna are 56 cents.

The excessive fat, the high price and the sodium nitrite are enough reasons to scratch such foods from your regular menu. Occasionally, when you may want a bacon or ham flavor, you can seek out those made without sodium nitrite. And that's one place where label reading becomes important.

Most processed products containing sodium nitrite will list the additive on the label, but not if the product has been repackaged at the store or if it has not been sold in interstate commerce. It's reasonable to assume that in the absence of an ingredient statement to the contrary, all of the following contain sodium nitrite: bacon, ham, hot dogs, bologna, salami, liverwurst, luncheon meats, beef jerky, chicken hot dogs, turkey ham, pastrami, corned beef, smoked and pickled tongue, cured sausage, some fresh sausage, smoked fish such as lox, Nova Scotia salmon, whitefish and sturgeon, salt pork.

And don't be fooled if a sign says these meats contain no sodium nitrate (with an *a*). Few processed meats do anymore, but they still contain the nitrites (with an *i*). Nevertheless, each year it becomes easier to find nitrite-free products. Three years ago there was only one place to buy nitrite-free bacon in Washington, D.C. Now there are a dozen or more. And anyone can purchase nitrite-free country ham from the Prospect Store, 10312 U. S. Highway 42, Prospect, Kentucky 40059, and Kites in Wolftown, Virginia 22748.

DES is still permitted as a growth stimulant in cattle, even though in large amounts it has caused a rare form of cancer in some female offspring, and infertility in some male offspring, of women who took it during pregnancy. You have three alternatives: avoid beef entirely and stick to chicken and fish; buy organically grown beef; stay away from beef liver, where most chemical residues end up.

If you don't want to eat ice cream or yogurt with artificial ingredients, there are more choices on the market today than a few years ago. Yogurt and frozen yogurt must list their ingredients on the label. Soon ice cream will have an ingredient statement, too, with one ridiculous exception. Because of the powerful dairy lobby, ice cream, along with butter and natural cheese, does not have to list the presence of artificial coloring. The new FDA regulation that is scheduled to take effect July 1, 1979, requiring ingredient labeling for ice cream, will not change that fact. The FDA has told ice cream manufacturers that they ought to disclose the source of the coloring, but the agency can't force them to do so.

With as many chemicals as most commercial ice creams contain, it hardly seems newsworthy that manufacturers wanted to degrade the product further. But their desire to do away with one of the few natural ingredients left in ice cream—milk!—made headlines across the country. The manufacturers wanted to substitute casein, a chemically derived milk protein, because it would have saved them about 2½ percent in costs. Would the people who buy ice cream ever see these savings? Even the International Association of Ice Cream Manufacturers says it's "doubtful." And don't be taken in by the ice cream label that trumpets "All natural flavor." That doesn't make the rest of the ice cream natural.

On the subject of flavors, a product can call itself "strawberry" ice cream or "orange" drink if it is flavored naturally. If it contains more natural than artificial flavor, it must say "strawberry flavored" ice cream. If it contains more artificial than natural flavor, then it must say "artificially flavored strawberry" ice cream.

But be on your guard for another trend to the "natural" bandwagon. Many products are calling themselves "natural" because the additives they contain come from natural sources: guar gum, locust bean, hydrolized cereal solids.

I have just one simple rule of thumb for determining the naturalness of a product. If I can't make it in my kitchen, it doesn't fit my idea of natural.

Just as it's easier these days to buy more natural ice cream, there are a lot more whole-grain breads available with natural ingredients. No, they won't last in the bread box for three weeks, like white so-called bread that makes better spitballs than sandwiches. But you can keep them for many days in the refrigerator (toast to freshen when the bread gets firm) and much longer in the freezer. Usually it's impossible to tell by looking if the product is 100 percent whole grain or just colored with caramel to make you think so. But the list of ingredients will tell you. If any ingredient listed is "white flour," "enriched flour," "wheat flour," or "sprouted wheat," the bread is *not* whole grain.

That phrase "wheat flour" has been turning up more and more on bread products and it's easy to believe the term is meant to confuse you into thinking the bread is whole wheat. A whole-grain bread will have only whole grains in it. For 100 percent whole-wheat bread, look for "*whole*-wheat flour."

Since ingredients are listed in order of predominance, if the package lists "wheat flour" and then "whole-wheat flour," there is more wheat (white) flour in the product than whole-wheat flour.

With the rage for fiber in the diet, whole-grain breads are a good way to add it, but breads containing powdered cellulose are not. The source of powdered cellulose is likely to be ground-up trees, or wood pulp, which has been chemically treated. The best-known "bread product," touted as high in fiber, is ITT Continental Baking Company's Fresh Horizons Special Formula bread.

The company insists that powdered cellulose is not wood pulp, or, as Senator George McGovern called it during a Senate hearing, "sawdust." But all of ITT's protestations will not change the fact that the powdered cellulose in the bread product started out as a tree. And there are no scientific studies that demonstrate the safety of eating large amounts of wood pulp over a long period of time.

When I wrote a story in *The Washington Post* in 1976 which explained that the powdered cellulose in Fresh Horizons once grew in a forest, ITT threatened legal action, claiming inaccuracies in the story, a threat they never carried out.

When Dr. Art Ulene and I repeated similar information on his "Feeling Fine" segment of the "Today" show the following summer, ITT made the same charges and asked for an opportunity to appear on the show. Dr. Ulene agreed and said he would include some film showing how a loaf of Fresh Horizons was made, from tree to finished product. At first ITT said OK, but the company changed its mind just as the film crew was about to shoot the mixing of the ingredients in the bakery.

Fresh Horizons, which costs 10 cents more per loaf than ordinary bread, must call itself "Special Formula bread" because it is not really bread according to FDA standards. Fresh Horizons is 46 percent water and 7.5 percent wood pulp. Regular bread contains between 35 and 36 percent water and, of course, no wood pulp.

Don't buy breads containing "powdered cellulose." When you want to add fiber to your diet, eat whole grains, fruits and vegetables.

Label reading is also crucial when you approach the cheese display. It is also confusing and time-consuming. But reading labels is the only way you won't have a fast one put over on you, unless you stick with natural cheeses.

The best, and supposedly most expensive, is natural cheese. It has the highest content of dairy product, often called milk fat, and the least amount of moisture (water). You are most likely to find uncolored cheese in this category. Almost without exception all processed cheeses are artificially colored whether or not the label says so.

Pasteurized processed cheese comes next, with a lower milk-fat content and more water. Then pasteurized processed cheese *food* with even less milk fat and even more water. Finally, pasteurized processed cheese *spread* has the least milk fat of the four and the greatest amount of water.

There is one additional class of cheese products called "imitation." This includes diet cheeses and filled cheeses, the latter containing no milk products.

Since milk fat is the costliest ingredient in cheese, the most expensive cheeses should be the natural ones, but that is definitely not the case. The price of processed cheeses is directly related to the amount of packaging, shaping or cutting. Things such as Cheez Kisses, which are made of cheese spread, cost over 50 cents more per pound than a natural aged sharp Cheddar. If your store has unit pricing, so that you can compare the cost per pound, you will spot that in a minute.

As for those individually wrapped cheese slices (most of which are artificially colored anyway), once again you are paying someone to do the wrapping. Almost any time someone else does the slicing, chunking, shaping, cutting or separating, it will cost more.

Aside from all thought of value, price and artificial color, there is not a single processed cheese that can hold a candle to a natural cheese when it comes to taste.

A package of chicken parts—breasts, wings, drumsticks, etc.—is far more expensive than a whole chicken. Even a cut-up chicken, which usually costs a few cents more per pound than a whole chicken, is a better buy than chicken parts. Watch out for those "family packs" and other combinations that have more necks and backs than any normal chicken. They are not good buys.

And when it comes to another kind of poultry—turkey—read labels. Butterball turkeys contain no butter, just cheap vegetable oil. The best buy in turkeys is frozen, plain. The best-tasting are fresh; they cost more but are well worth it.

There are some rare exceptions to the cost of parts versus the whole: pieces of canned fruits, vegetables and nuts are cheaper than the whole. In other words, whole peaches, even peach halves, cost more than peach slices; whole green beans are more expensive than cut; walnut chips are cheaper than walnut halves.

And don't ignore the volume-versus-weight game in the produce section. A lot of produce is sold by the piece, not the pound. Some pieces weigh as much as a pound more than others, but cost the same. So take the time to weigh several heads of cauliflower or baskets of cherry tomatoes if they are sold by volume, to find the best buy.

If supermarkets insist on packaging produce and you find that the apples come only six or more to the package, but all you need is three, either open the package and take out what you want, or ask the produce man to do it for you. If the produce department frowns on this, take it up with the store manager. You might remind him or her that the store is in business to serve customers, not to make them buy more than they can use. If none of these techniques works, take your business elsewhere.

If you don't know what an ingredient is in the prepared foods you wish to buy, you have two choices: leave the product on the shelf or write the manufacturer and ask him. If he doesn't respond, drop the product like a hot potato. What does the company have to hide?

SUPERMARKET ALTERNATIVES

You may have better luck understanding labels in a natural-food store, but you also may be paying a stiff price for some products that are exactly the same as those in the ordinary supermarket. Do some comparative shopping. There are even some instances where the natural-food store offers a better buy. At the one in which I shop, powdered yeast, free of BHT, and unprocessed bran are much, much cheaper. So are some of the grains such as buckwheat groats and bulgur, as well as sunflower seeds, which come unsalted as do all the nuts. (Toasted, unsalted sunflower seeds are a delicious snack!)

Often the natural-food stores are the only source of nitrite-free processed meats in a city, and if you like those foods it's worth the extra money.

Another alternative to supermarket shopping is the farmer's market or roadside truck. These are wonderful places to buy fresh produce from nearby fields and orchards. They help keep local farmers in business and provide city dwellers with the taste of real food, sometimes at savings, seldom for more than the going supermarket price.

These markets are doing extremely well for the same reason people are turning away from convenience foods. Two surveys conducted by both ends of the food chain, a farmers' group and a supermarket industry organization, show this very clearly.

Food Marketing Institute, the trade association for the supermarket industry, has been studying shoppers' habits since 1974. Every six months one of the questions its asks shoppers is whether they have cut down on the amount of convenience foods they have purchased. The numbers who have cut down have been increasing.

The Agriculture Council of America asked shoppers if they were satisfied or dissatisfied with the quality and nutritional value of the food they bought. Fifty percent said they were *not* satisfied. Eighty-six percent said they would prefer less convenience packaging and would welcome the opportunity to buy more in bulk. Eighty-nine percent would like to see more direct farmer-to-consumer marketing. Most people think this will save money; some would prefer it because they could get better quality.

In a 1976 survey of the shopping habits of working versus nonworking women, one of the most interesting statistics of all turned up. More working than nonworking women said they "never" bought frozen TV dinners, prepared main-dish entrees, vegetables, dessert or instant coffee. Apparently, no one has ever been able to sell them a bill of goods about the convenience of convenience foods.

Working and nonworking women alike who did not use such products said:

"If I relied on convenience foods I couldn't afford it."

"I don't like the way they taste."

"They aren't good for you."

"There are too many additives, so I avoid them."

"They all taste alike."

DIETARY GOALS

When you consider the chemicals fed to animals, the pesticides sprayed on the produce, you understand the subtitle of the book: Cooking with the "most" natural, additive-free ingredients you can buy. Nothing is really "pure and simple." And if you are like me, you do the best you can. You get rid of as many hazards as you do not care to live with. You make some compromises.

I use sugar for special-occasion desserts because I still believe there is room for a moderate amount of it in the diet. I also think there is room for an occasional fried dish, but not for lunch every day, or even once a week.

I guess I probably subscribe to the general outline of the Senate Nutrition Committee's report "Dietary Goals for the United States." The report was made public in January, 1977, and has become extremely controversial because it recommends drastic changes in dietary habits in this country. Almost every special-interest group has attacked it: the cattlemen, the sugar association, egg producers, dairy industry, fruit and vegetable canners and the American Medical Association. Why? Because the recommendations call for a drop in the consumption of beef, eggs, sugar, dairy products (particularly those high in fat), canned fruits and vegetables.

How did the AMA get into the act? It's hard to say, except that the association strongly suggests in its critique of "Dietary Goals" that disease should be cured, not prevented.

While I do not agree completely with the Nutrition Committee's dietary recommendations, they provide the most comprehensive guide to eating better for a longer and healthier life ever put out by the federal government. The Committee had no ax to grind.

These are the six goals outlined by the Nutrition Committee report:

1. An increase in consumption of complex carbohydrates so they account for 55 to 60 percent of the caloric intake.
2. Reduction in sugar consumption by 40 percent so that it accounts for about 15 percent of total caloric intake.
3. Reduction in overall fat consumption by 10 percent so that it accounts for about 30 percent of total calories.
4. Reduction in saturated-fat consumption to account for about 10 percent of total calories; and balance that with polyunsaturated and monosaturated fats, which should account for about 10 percent of the calories each.
5. Reduction in cholesterol consumption to about 300 milligrams a day.
6. Reduction in salt consumption by 50 to 85 percent.

Since diet-related illness—heart disease, certain forms of cancer, diabetes and obesity—is believed to be the major cause of death and disability in the United States, Americans have to start changing their eating habits. Moderation is the key, so I would be the first to say that many of the recipes in the book are not appropriate as a steady diet.

But for festive or important occasions, for parties and celebrations, why not? If you eat fruit for dessert five nights a week, there's nothing wrong with a mousse or a cake on Saturday. If you have plain broiled entrees at family meals every weekday night, a casserole of chicken, sour cream and wine for Sunday dinner is just fine.

Well-prepared basic ingredients are far more satisfying than the highly processed foods so you tend to eat less of them. Psychologically, it is because you are satisfied by them. Physiologically, foods high in complex carbohydrates—fruits, vegetables, whole grains—add more bulk to your diet than refined carbohydrates—candy, cookies and other sweets—so you are more quickly satiated.

Ironically, using natural or barely processed ingredients (frozen plain vegetables) does not cost more than using highly processed foods.

NEW TRENDS IN COOKING

Along with the turning away from factory-produced convenience is an increase in the purchase of kitchen equipment designed to make cooking from scratch quicker and easier. From the costly food processors which make short work of onion chopping, meat grinding, etc., to the slow cookers which make it possible to simmer a stew all day while you are at work, sales have increased dramatically.

Attendance at cooking schools is high. Men are going more often, too, as young households share more of the kitchen chores.

Frankly, it had never occurred to me to combine the serious aspects of my work as food editor of *The Washington Post* and reporter for WRC-TV—economics, safety and health—with my love of well-prepared foods and good cooking. It was my agent's idea!

This chapter is the serious part. Doubtless it will anger some people. There will be attempts to discredit it, but I'll stick with erring on the side of safety. And anyone who can argue that factory-prepared food tastes as good as what you make at home with the best ingredients either was born without taste buds or has had them numbed by countless encounters with the technological marvels of laboratory-created foods.

For those who like the ready-when-you-need-it quality of some convenience foods, a chapter has been included on making your own. These recipes are as convenient as anything you can buy, are practically free of additives and always cost less than those you buy ready-made when comparable ingredients are used. You can make them when you have the time and put them away to use when you are in a hurry.

Some of the convenience-food recipes are included not only for convenience but also to show you how easy it is to make certain foods at home such as your own meat sauce, frozen yogurt, mincemeat with real meat, flavored gelatins, and beef and chicken stock or broth (the words are interchangeable). Most of the recipes in this chapter are for family meals when you are in a rush, though some of them certainly fit properly into entertaining menus. There is a chapter on meatless main dishes, making it easier to entertain your lacto-ovo vegetarian (those who eat egg and milk products but not meats) friends and relatives. Everyone seems to have at least one these days. Dozens of recipes in other chapters are meatless as well.

These recipes are an eclectic collection of dishes with which I have been experimenting and entertaining for the last five years. There has been no particular effort to include "one of each kind." Rather, there is an almost visible thread running through them which traces my interest in new ethnic foods—Chinese, particularly Szechuan, Middle Eastern and Mexican—and my increasing reliance on vegetables and fruits.

In other words, the recipes are simply those I have served that our guests have enjoyed. Coming to dinner at our house involves being a guinea pig most of the time. So far no complaints.

In my metamorphosis from user of convenience foods to lover of the basics, I have learned many new things. They include changes and substitutions that must be made in order to convert ingredients in the following recipes:

- Substitute brown rice for white-brown rice. It takes 45 minutes to cook brown rice, so just start it earlier. When cooked, it has a nut-like flavor and doesn't look much browner than white rice.
- Substitute honey or molasses for sugar. It does not work for everything, and certainly not in a light cake. Honey and molasses give a moister, chewier, heavier texture and also may cause excessive browning.

  For every 1¼ cups sugar, use 1 cup honey and decrease liquid by ¼ cup. If there is no liquid in the recipe, add ¼ cup of flour. Unless sour cream or sour milk is used in the recipe, add a pinch of baking soda.

  For every ¾ cup sugar, use 1 cup unsulfured molasses. Decrease liquid by ¼ cup for each cup of molasses, omit any baking powder and add ½ teaspoon baking soda.

- Substitute unbleached white flour for bleached all-purpose on a one-to-one ratio.
- Substitute whole-wheat for white all-purpose flour. For every cup of white use ¾ cup whole-wheat. Reduce shortening by using two tablespoons for every three called for. Add a tablespoon or two of liquid for cakes, slightly more for breads.
- Substitute fresh herbs for dried. Use three times as much fresh. If a recipe calls for 1 tablespoon of dried dill, use 3 tablespoons fresh. This is just a guide because the amount you use will depend in part on the age, and therefore potency, of the dried herbs with which you usually cook.
- Use fresh ginger. When you find it buy a large piece; and after you have used what you need, freeze the rest. When you need fresh ginger, thin slices can be cut quite easily from the frozen piece.
- Use Chinese or Japanese soy sauce. Use the Chinese light (unless the recipe directs otherwise) if you can get it. If not, use the Japanese brand found in most supermarkets. *Don't* use the American brand; it has more "junk" than the others and is much saltier.
- Substitute pasteurized heavy cream for ultrapasteurized heavy cream. The dairy industry has figured out a way to make heavy cream last four times as long as any self-respecting cream should through ultrapasteurization. Also, many people complain that ultrapasteurized cream does not whip properly.
- Substitute unsalted for salted butter. First, it is less likely to be colored. Then it is more likely to be fresh. Unsalted butter is made from fresh cream instead of cream that has turned. Salt helps to disguise the soured taste.
- Learn to use less salt. While some recipes call for a specific amount of salt, less can be used, or it can be eliminated entirely except where it performs a specific function, such as in the recipe for making gravlax (marinated salmon).

To make it easier to entertain without the use of convenience foods, most of the recipes in the book can be prepared ahead of time and either frozen weeks in advance or refrigerated for one or more days before serving.

While freezing does not improve the flavor of anything, there are many dishes whose quality is not noticeably affected. Cooking ahead and refrigerating most dishes will not affect their taste or texture. Dishes which may be frozen are marked with an *F*; dishes which may be refrigerated are marked with an *R* plus a figure (*1, 2, 3*) indicating the number of days ahead they may be prepared and refrigerated.

Even in the recipes which require last-minute work, there are often steps that can be done ahead: washing, chopping, preparation of the sauce, braising or initial sautéing.

I have always found it immensely helpful to program the preparation of a party. First I work out the menu so that very few, possibly even none, of the dishes are last-minute. Then comes a cooking schedule since I must fit it in on nights and weekends.

I make two, sometimes three, grocery lists. One is for the ingredients which are bought well in advance, either because they won't spoil or because they will be used in recipes that are prepared ahead. That list includes the wine for dinner and cocktails. Before dinner we serve as much wine as hard liquor, white wine being the great favorite. The second list is for ingredients that may be bought the day before the party. The final one is for those ingredients that will suffer if they are even one day old.

Then I write a list of all the dishes and serving pieces that will be needed. It's much easier than standing at the drawer and scratching my head, wondering what I ought to serve the mousse on!

I also make note of when things must be defrosted and when they must go in the oven.

I tend to get so interested in conversations at parties that without my lists the food might never make it to the table. The trick still is getting it all there at the same time, and my time and temperature information keeps me out of trouble.

I find it rather exciting that cooking this way means not only less expensive but more nutritious and better-tasting food. But maybe the greatest thrill of all is knowing that even if I haven't beaten the system, at least we are on an equal footing.

REMEMBER THE CODE
BY THE RECIPE TITLES . . .

F   means the dish may be frozen.

R   means it may be made ahead and refrigerated; the number tells you for how many days.

For instance: F / R2—the dish may be either frozen or refrigerated for two days.

A FEW "CONVENIENCE" RECIPES

℧

BREAKFAST NOG

2 servings

2 ripe bananas   2 eggs
1½ cups milk   1 teaspoon vanilla

Cut banana in quarters and place in electric blender with remaining ingredients. Cover and blend until smooth.

℧

INSTANT BREAKFAST

1 serving

1 cup cold milk   3 tablespoons undiluted orange
1 egg   juice concentrate

Place ingredients in blender and blend at high speed until frothy. Serve immediately.
(Including froth, this makes 2 cups.)

℧

INSTANT COCOA

Makes 6 cups of mix

4 cups instant nonfat dry milk   1¼ cups or more sugar
¾ cup unsweetened cocoa   ⅛ teaspoon salt
  powder

Combine ingredients and stir well. Store in tightly covered container in cool, dry place. To make instant cocoa, stir mixture. Place

3½ tablespoons of mix in cup and pour in a little of 1 cup boiling water, stirring well to dissolve mixture. Continue pouring water and stirring. Serve immediately.

ॐ

HOT MOCHA MIX

Makes approximately 6 cups of mix

1 cup unsweetened cocoa
2 cups sugar
4 cups nonfat dry milk powder

¾ cup instant coffee powder
1 vanilla bean or 3 tablespoons
    dried orange peel

Combine all ingredients and mix well. Store in airtight container for at least a week before using so that flavors can blend.

To serve, stir mix well. Place 3 tablespoons of mix in cup. Pour in a little of 6 ounces of boiling water and stir well to dissolve mix. Continue pouring in water and stirring and serve immediately.

ॐ

CINNAMON SUGAR

2 tablespoons cinnamon   1 cup sugar

Mix and store tightly covered. Use for toast, etc.

ॐ

SEASONED SALT

Makes approximately 1 cup

1 cup salt
2½ teaspoons paprika
2 teaspoons dry mustard
1½ teaspoons oregano

1 teaspoon garlic powder
    (or to taste)
½ teaspoon onion powder

Mix together and store in airtight container. Use to season oil and vinegar dressing, meats, fish and vegetables.

〜

CURRY POWDER

So many different spices can go into a curry powder: ginger, coriander, cayenne, cumin, cardamom, chiles, cinnamon, fennel, mace, black pepper, mustard and of course turmeric, which gives curry the golden color, are some of them. Here is one suggestion for a curry powder, not particularly fiery, but it can be heated up with cayenne.

2 tablespoons each ground coriander, black pepper, cumin, *chile* *
    and turmeric
1¼ teaspoons ground ginger

Mix well and store in airtight container away from light.
Always bring the full flavor of the curry out by cooking it in the dish. It is not enough just to stir it in.

〜

FIVE SPICE POWDER

This is a Chinese seasoning which differs in content, depending on the cookbook. If you cannot purchase it, you can make your own by mixing equal parts of:

Anise	Cinnamon	Clove
Fennel	Black Pepper	

Since some of these spices are not available ground, you may have to grind them yourself. A pepper mill will work, but it's a bit slow. An electric grinder makes it a little easier.

---

* This is pure *chile* (with an *e*) powder found in Spanish grocery stores. Chili (with an *i*) powder is a mixture of several spices.

❧

R3

FIVE SPICE DIP

Makes approximately 3 cups

The unusual ingredient is the Five Spice Powder, a Chinese mixture.

2 cups sour cream
½ teaspoon Five Spice Powder
  (page 39)

½ cup peanuts, chopped
  coarsely
½ cup chopped chutney
1 tablespoon chopped onion

If serving immediately, combine all ingredients. Otherwise, combine all ingredients but peanuts. Just before serving, add peanuts. Serve with an assortment of raw vegetables. Will keep a week.

❧

GRANOLA

Makes about 10 cups

Grains, nuts, seeds and dried fruits, sweetened with honey or molasses, are called granola when the grains are toasted before the other ingredients are added. Granolas are rich in protein, iron and *calories*. They will keep for weeks when stored in the refrigerator.

3 cups rolled oats
1½ cups wheat germ
½ cup dry skim-milk powder
1 cup slivered or coarsely
  chopped almonds
½ cup sesame seeds

1 cup hulled sunflower seeds
½ cup vegetable oil
¼ to ½ cup honey
1 cup raisins
½ cup dried apricots, cut up

Toast the oats in a shallow pan at 300 degrees for 15 minutes. In a large bowl combine the wheat germ, skim-milk powder, almonds, sesame and sunflower seeds. Heat the oil and honey just until warm. Combine with mixture in the bowl. Combine contents of bowl with toasted oats and spread in several shallow pans in thin layer. Continue toasting, stirring occasionally, for 15 minutes more, or until ingredients are toasted. Spoon into large container; add raisins and apricots. Cool and store in tightly covered container in the refrigerator. Serve with milk or yogurt.

NOTE: My son likes this granola better with roasted, unsalted peanuts. You can vary it any way that suits your taste.

❦

R / F

GARLIC BUTTER

This will keep as long as butter keeps in the refrigerator. It can be cut into individual portions and frozen for several months.

½ cup (¼ pound) butter, softened
2 to 3 cloves garlic, minced or put through garlic press
2 tablespoons minced parsley

Combine ingredients and beat until fluffy. Cover tightly and refrigerate or freeze. Use for garlic bread or on vegetables, or over broiled fish or beef.

❦

R

HONEY BUTTER

Makes 1 cup

½ cup honey   ½ cup soft butter

Blend honey and butter. Store in refrigerator. Serve with hot biscuits or pancakes.

ᛒ

R

BLENDER MAYONNAISE

Makes approximately 1¾ cups

If you want to make mayonnaise at home and have a blender, it is quick work indeed. It is not quite as good as the mayonnaise beaten by hand, but much better than the sweetened, chemically preserved, commercial product. This will keep 2 or 3 weeks, well covered, in the refrigerator.

1 egg	1¼ cups salad oil, or combination of salad and olive oil
1 teaspoon dry mustard	
½ teaspoon salt (scant)	2 tablespoons lemon juice, or half lemon juice and half white wine vinegar
Dash cayenne pepper	

Place the egg, mustard, salt, cayenne and ¼ cup oil in blender. Blend at high speed until completely mixed. With blender still running, take off center of cover or cover itself and slowly pour in ½ cup of oil. After it is completely blended (it may be necessary to turn off motor and mix mayonnaise a little with scraper), blend in lemon juice thoroughly. Then slowly add remaining oil, turning motor off and on as necessary to blend completely.

NOTE: Tarragon vinegar may also be used.

ᛒ

R

INSTANT CHEESE SAUCE

1½ pounds Gruyère cheese, finely grated	¾ cup sour cream
	Salt to taste

Mix cheese and sour cream; season to taste with salt. Pack in tightly covered container and refrigerate.

To use, spread mixture on broiled fish run under broiler to melt cheese, or spoon into piping hot split baked potatoes, or mix with hot mashed potatoes, or spread on toasted bread and broil until cheese melts, or spoon over scrambled eggs or into omelet before folding, or spoon over hot vegetables.

This will keep as long as the sour cream keeps. Check the carton for the expiration date.

ૐ

R /F

CREAM SAUCE MIX FOR VEGETABLES

Makes 2 cups

½ cup butter	2 tablespoons onion powder
½ cup flour	2 teaspoons salt
½ cup nonfat dry milk powder	¼ teaspoon pepper

Cut the butter into the flour along with remaining ingredients, until mixture is very crumbly. Refrigerate or, if desired, keep in the freezer along with frozen vegetables with which the mixture is used.

To use: combine 2 cups of vegetables with ½ cup water and bring to boil. Cover pan and cook vegetables until they are tender but still crisp. Length of time will depend on the vegetables. Stir in 3 tablespoons of sauce mix and cook, stirring until sauce thickens. Season to taste with salt. Serve.

Vegetables and sauce can be seasoned with herbs: peas with oregano; green beans with basil; carrots with dill. Allow ¾ teaspoon dried herb for each 2 cups of vegetables; 2 to 2½ teaspoons fresh herbs.

ೞ

R

THOUSAND ISLAND DRESSING

Makes 1½ cups

1 cup Mayonnaise (page 42) 1 tablespoon pickle relish
½ cup chili sauce

Combine ingredients and store in refrigerator indefinitely. For variation, add finely chopped green olives, grated onion or minced green pepper.

ೞ

CHEESE SALAD SEASONING

Makes approximately 8 tablespoons

¼ cup dry grated cheese (Parmesan, Romano, Cheddar) ¼ teaspoon black pepper
2 tablespoons sesame seeds 2 teaspoons paprika
2 teaspoons salt 1 teaspoon celery seed
  ½ teaspoon garlic powder

Combine ingredients and mix well. Store in airtight container. To use, sprinkle on salads or mix with salad dressing, about 2 teaspoons to a cup of dressing.

ೞ

SALAD DRESSING MIX

Enough for 8 cups liquid

2 to 4 teaspoons salt 1 teaspoon black pepper
1 teaspoon dried minced garlic 1 teaspoon sugar
4 teaspoons instant minced onion 1 teaspoon paprika

Combine ingredients and store, tightly covered, in cool, dry place. To use, combine 2 tablespoons water with ¼ cup vinegar. Stir in 1½ teaspoons season mix and then ⅔ cup salad oil. Beat well or shake in tightly covered bottle. Makes 1 cup salad dressing.

FRENCH DRESSING MIX

Enough for 8 cups dressing

2 to 4 teaspoons salt	1 tablespoon plus 1 teaspoon
1 tablespoon plus 1 teaspoon	dry mustard
paprika	½ teaspoon black pepper

Combine ingredients and store in tightly covered container at room temperature.

To make French dressing: combine 1 tablespoon of mix with ¼ cup vinegar or lemon juice and ¾ cup salad oil.

Variations:

For garlic French dressing, add 1 crushed clove garlic.

For curry French dressing, add ¼ to ½ teaspoon curry powder.

For blue cheese dressing, stir in 2 teaspoons water with ¾ cup crumbled blue cheese.

VINAIGRETTE DRESSING

Makes 1 cup

1 tablespoon French Dressing Mix (above)	2 tablespoons finely chopped dill pickle
¾ cup salad oil	2 teaspoons chopped chives
¼ cup vinegar	1 hard-cooked egg, chopped

Combine oil and vinegar with mix and shake well. Add remaining ingredients and shake again.

❧

MIXED PICKLING SPICE

Makes ⅔ cup

4 cinnamon sticks, each about 3 inches long
1 piece dried ginger root, 1 inch long
2 tablespoons mustard seed
2 teaspoons whole allspice
2 teaspoons whole black peppercorns

2 teaspoons whole cloves
2 teaspoons dill seed
2 teaspoons coriander seed
2 teaspoons whole mace, crumbled
8 bay leaves, crumbled
1 whole dried red pepper, 1½ inches long, chopped

Wrap cinnamon sticks and ginger root in clean cloth. Pound with a mallet or hammer until finely crumbled; discard stringy part of ginger. Add to the remaining ingredients and stir well. Store in airtight container.

❧

POULTRY SEASONING

Makes scant ½ cup

2 tablespoons dried marjoram
2 tablespoons dried parsley
2 tablespoons dried savory

1 tablespoon dried sage
1½ teaspoons dried thyme

Combine ingredients and store in airtight container. Use as you would any commercially prepared poultry seasoning.

❦

SHAKE IT AND BAKE IT

Enough for 6 pounds of chicken

1 cup flour
2 teaspoons salt
1 teaspoon pepper
½ cup cracker crumbs

1 teaspoon herbs (thyme,
   oregano, basil or a mixture)
Milk or water

Combine dry ingredients, stirring to mix. Use half the mixture for 3 pounds of chicken. Reserve remainder in a tightly covered container. Moisten the chicken with milk or water. Shake chicken pieces with mix, a few at a time, in paper bag. Bake in greased shallow pan at 350 degrees for 45 minutes to 1 hour.

❦

R / F

ITALIAN COATING MIX

1 quart fine bread crumbs
½ cup finely grated Romano or
   Cheddar cheese
3 small cloves garlic, crushed

½ cup vegetable oil
1 cup fresh parsley, chopped
1 teaspoon salt
1 teaspoon pepper

Combine all ingredients and mix thoroughly; freeze. Spoon out amount needed to pat on chicken pieces. Place a single layer of coated food in shallow pan; cover with foil and bake at 350 degrees 45 to 60 minutes. Five minutes before baking time is up, remove foil and brown.

This mixture keeps for a week in the refrigerator; in the freezer it does not become solid, but remains spoonable.

Can be used to coat fish, veal and chicken.

ᦵᖋᕽ

HELP FOR HAMBURGERS

Five 1-cup servings

This is Oriental-style.

1 pound ground beef
3⅓ cups hot water
2¼ cups instant rice

2 tablespoons instant minced
  onion
¼ cup soy sauce
Salt to taste

Brown meat in skillet; drain off fat. Add hot water, rice, onion and soy sauce. Mix well and bring to boiling point. Cook over medium-high heat until most of liquid has evaporated, 10 to 15 minutes. Season to taste with salt, if desired.

ᦵᖋᕽ

INSTANT STUFFING

4 servings

Makes use of leftover bread ends, stale slices and crust.

4 cups large bread crumbs or
  cubes
1 teaspoon dried minced onion
1 teaspoon dried parsley

½ teaspoon thyme
Dash sage
3 tablespoons butter
½ cup Chicken or Beef Stock
  (pages 89, 90)

Place bread crumbs or cubes on a baking sheet and heat at 350 degrees for 5 to 10 minutes, until dry. Place in tightly covered container. When you have 4 cups of crumbs, stir in onion, parsley, thyme and sage. Cover and store in cupboard; it will keep for weeks.

To make stuffing, melt butter; add crumb mixture and toss to coat.

Slowly add stock and mix gently but well. Cook over low heat until hot, or place in baking dish and bake at 350 degrees for 30 minutes. If mixture is too dry, add more stock or water. Season with salt and pepper and serve.

NOTE: If you prefer to use freshly chopped onion and parsley, add them when you combine stuffing mixture with butter. For 2 cups of crumbs, allow 1 tablespoon chopped onion and 1 tablespoon chopped parsley.

ᔥ

R / F

MEAT SAUCE

One-third of recipe serves 4 to 6 people

3 pounds ground beef	3 (8-ounce) cans tomato sauce
3 large onions, chopped	Salt and pepper to taste
3 green peppers, seeded and chopped	1 tablespoon oregano
	1½ teaspoons basil
6 cloves garlic, finely chopped	6 tablespoons coffee
3 (1-pound) cans tomatoes	1½ cups dry red wine
3 (6-ounce) cans tomato paste	

Brown meat in skillet, stirring to break up pieces. Push meat to side and sauté onion, peppers and garlic until onion is soft. Add remaining ingredients and simmer for 1½ hours, or until mixture is thick.

Serve over spaghetti or your favorite pasta. One third of recipe is enough for 1 pound of spaghetti.

The rest of the sauce can be frozen in portions suitable for your family's use in other recipes.

To make sloppy joes:

Combine 2 cups of meat sauce with one teaspoon Worcestershire sauce and hot pepper sauce to taste. Serve over buns.

To make chili:

Combine 2 cups meat sauce with a 15-ounce can of kidney beans and 1 tablespoon chili powder.

&

OATMEAL COOKIE MIX

8 dozen

3 cups sifted flour	2 teaspoons salt
2½ cups sugar	1 cup shortening
1 teaspoon baking soda	3 cups rolled oats
1 teaspoon baking powder	

Sift together flour, sugar, soda, baking powder and salt. Cut in shortening until mix resembles cornmeal. Add rolled oats and mix well. Store in tightly covered container at room temperature.

To make 2 to 2½ dozen cookies:

2 cups oatmeal cookie mix	1 tablespoon milk
1 egg	1 teaspoon vanilla

Place mix in bowl, add egg, milk and vanilla. Mix well. Drop from teaspoon onto greased baking sheets. Bake at 375 degrees for 12 to 15 minutes, until golden. Remove from sheet and store.

Variations:

½ cup chopped nuts, or	½ cup chopped dates
½ cup raisins, or	

❧

R / F

SLICE AND BAKE COOKIES

Approximately 4 dozen

½ cup sugar
½ cup shortening
1 egg yolk
1½ teaspoons vanilla extract
1½ cups sifted flour

¼ teaspoon salt
½ teaspoon baking powder
3 tablespoons milk
1-ounce square unsweetened
   chocolate, melted

Cream sugar and shortening. Stir in yolk and vanilla. Combine flour, salt and baking powder. Stir alternately with milk into sugar mixture to make soft dough.

Divide dough in half. Add chocolate to one half; mix thoroughly. On wax paper roll out each half into rectangles ⅛ inch thick. Turn white dough onto chocolate dough with chocolate dough extending ½ inch beyond white dough along edge toward which you will roll. Remove wax paper; roll up like jelly roll.

Wrap in wax paper; refrigerate or freeze, if desired. To finish cookies, cut roll into thin slices, ⅛ to ¼ inch thick. Bake at 375 degrees for 8 to 10 minutes, depending on thickness of cookies.

Dough keeps indefinitely in the freezer and for a couple of weeks in refrigerator.

❧

R

BRAN OATMEAL MUFFIN MIX

8 dozen medium muffins

2 cups boiling water
2 cups 100 percent bran
1 cup shortening
3 cups sugar (white or brown or
   mixed)
4 eggs

1 quart buttermilk
5 cups flour
1 teaspoon salt
5 teaspoons baking soda
4 cups uncooked oatmeal

Pour boiling water over the bran and set aside while mixing the rest of the ingredients. Cream sugar and shortening. Add eggs, buttermilk, flour, salt and soda. Add cereals last. Use some of mix if desired, refrigerate remainder. Pour into well-greased medium muffin tins until ¾ full. Bake 15 to 20 minutes in a preheated 375-degree oven. For batter just out of the refrigerator, bake 20 to 25 minutes at the same temperature.

Raisins, nuts or dates can be added, but just before baking only.

This can be refrigerated up to 3 months.

❧

MASTER BAKING MIX

Makes 7 cups

6 cups unbleached flour
2½ tablespoons double-action
baking powder
1½ teaspoons salt
¾ cup vegetable shortening *

Sift dry ingredients together. Cut in shortening until mixture is crumbly. Store in tightly covered container in cupboard.

❧

MARMALADE NUT BREAD

1 loaf

3 cups Master Baking Mix
(above)
½ cup sugar
½ cup chopped nuts
1 egg, well beaten
1 cup milk
½ cup orange marmalade

Combine mix with sugar and nuts. Combine egg, milk and marmalade and blend. Add gradually to dry mixture, mixing only until flour

* If butter is used instead, mix must be stored in refrigerator.

is moistened. Turn into greased 9-x-5-x-3-inch loaf pan and bake at 350 degrees for 45 to 50 minutes. Cool in pan.

When cool, wrap bread in aluminum foil and allow to mellow at room temperature one day before slicing.

〜

DATE NUT MUFFINS

1 dozen

2 cups Master Baking Mix
  (page 52)
½ cup chopped pitted dates
¼ cup chopped nuts

1 egg, well beaten
½ to 1 tablespoon sugar
⅔ cup milk

Stir dates and nuts into mix. Stir egg, sugar and milk together. Add, all at once, to dry mixture. Stir only until flour is moistened—the batter will be lumpy. Fill medium-size greased muffin tins ⅔ full. Bake at 425 degrees for 15 to 18 minutes.

〜

BISCUIT MIX

Makes 13 cups

This can be used for waffles, pancakes, biscuits, and as a coating for chicken. Use it for anything for which you use packaged biscuit mix.

9 cups sifted flour
⅓ cup baking powder
1 cup plus 2 tablespoons
  nonfat milk solids

4 teaspoons salt
1¾ cups vegetable shortening

Sift all dry ingredients. Cut shortening into flour until mixture resembles coarse cornmeal. Store, well covered, in cool, dry place.

🙚

PANCAKES

Approximately twelve 4-inch pancakes

2 cups Biscuit Mix (page 53)   1 cup milk
2 eggs

Combine and beat until smooth. Bake pancakes on hot greased griddle until golden on both sides.

NOTE: To make fruit pancakes, add 1 cup blueberries, sliced strawberries, diced bananas or diced peaches to batter after it has been beaten.

🙚

WAFFLES

Three 9-inch waffles

2 cups Biscuit Mix (page 53)   1 egg
2 tablespoons oil   1½ cups milk

Combine ingredients and beat until smooth. Bake according to directions on waffle maker.

🙚

WRAP FOR HOT DOGS

Enough for 10 nitrite-free hot dogs, bratwurst or sausages

1 cup Biscuit Mix (page 53)   ¼ cup cold water

For onion flavor:

Mix 1½ teaspoons dried minced onion with water and allow to sit for a minute or two, then mix with Biscuit Mix. Form into ball. Knead a few times and roll out into 7½-×-8-inch rectangle. Cut into 10 rectangles.

For barbecue flavor:

Brush 2 tablespoons barbecue sauce over rolled-out dough.

For pizza flavor:

Combine ⅛ teaspoon garlic powder, 1½ teaspoons dried minced onion, ⅛ teaspoon oregano and 1 teaspoon dried parsley. Add to water and allow to sit for a minute or two.

For cheese flavor:

Sprinkle ½ cup grated cheese over rolled-out dough.

૪

PASTRY MIX

Makes 8 to 9 cups

6 cups sifted flour
1 tablespoon salt

1 (1-pound) can vegetable shortening (about 2½ cups)

Mix flour and salt in large bowl. Cut in shortening until mixture resembles coarse meal. Cover and store mix in cool place (it does not require refrigeration).

૪

PIE CRUSTS

For a 1-crust pie, use 2 to 4 tablespoons cold water and:

1¼ cups mix for 8-inch pie
1½ cups mix for 9-inch pie

1¾ cups mix for 10-inch pie

For a 2-crust pie, use ¼ to ⅓ cup cold water and:

2 to 2¼ cups mix for 8-inch pie

2¼ to 2½ cups mix for 9-inch pie

2½ to 2¾ cups mix for 10-inch pie

Measure mix into bowl; sprinkle on water, a little at a time, mixing quickly and evenly with fork until dough just holds together in a ball. Roll out as you would any pie crust.

❧

PUDDING AND PIE FILLING

Makes 10 cups

In earlier times these were known as cornstarch puddings. But that isn't a particularly appealing name.

3½ cups instant nonfat dry milk

¾ cup sugar

¾ cup cornstarch

Combine ingredients and store in tightly covered container in cool, dry place.

To make vanilla-flavored pudding: Stir the basic mix thoroughly and measure out 1 cup. Gradually add 2 cups of cold water; bring mixture to boil, stirring, over low heat. Mixture is boiling when it bubbles and plops. Add 1 teaspoon butter and ½ teaspoon vanilla. Stir until butter melts; pour into serving dishes and refrigerate. Makes four ½-cup servings.

For chocolate pudding: Combine mix and water as directed above. Stir in either one ounce of unsweetened chocolate or 4 tablespoons unsweetened cocoa and ½ teaspoon vanilla. Stir to mix well and pour into serving dishes. Refrigerate until set.

ℰ

R4

CRÈME FRAÎCHE

Makes approximately 1 pint

1 pint heavy cream for whipping *   2 tablespoons buttermilk

Pour cream into a jar. Stir in buttermilk. Cover loosely. Leave in a warm place, such as on top of stove, until cream thickens like yogurt. This can take as long as 4 days. Store in refrigerator for up to one week.

ℰ

F / R

MARY HUMELSINE'S MINCEMEAT

Makes approximately 7 quarts

This mincemeat, which Mary Humelsine makes every year for Christmas, is the real thing . . . it has meat in it. Mary's husband, Carl, is chairman of the board of Colonial Williamsburg.

2 pounds lean beef cubes   2 pounds brown sugar
1 pound beef suet   3 pints apple cider
5 pounds apples, peeled and   2 tablespoons cinnamon
  cored and cut in quarters   1 tablespoon nutmeg
2½ pounds raisins   1 tablespoon ground cloves
2 pounds currants   1 tablespoon allspice
½ pound citron, finely   Salt to taste
  chopped

---

* Do not use ultrapasteurized cream.

Cook the beef in water to cover until tender. Put cooked beef, suet and apples through coarse blade of meat grinder. Mix all ingredients together and pack tightly in sterilized jars (some liquid may be left over). Will keep indefinitely in refrigerator, up to a year, or can be frozen. Use in any recipe calling for mincemeat.

℧

F

FROZEN YOGURT

2 or 3 servings

This does not look like the frozen soft yogurts so popular right now, but it is delicious, contains much less sugar than the commercially produced brands, and it is all natural.

1 envelope unflavored gelatin	1 cup strawberries, blueberries,
1 tablespoon lemon juice	raspberries, cut-up peaches or
2 tablespoons water	nectarines, or 1 small cut-up
	banana
	1 tablespoon sugar
	1 cup plain yogurt

Soften gelatin in lemon juice and water. Heat either over hot water or over very low heat, stirring just until gelatin dissolves. Remove from heat. Add fruit, yogurt and sugar and mix lightly. Pour into blender and blend until mixture is fairly smooth. Little pieces of fruit are fine. They add bits of color and texture.

Pour mixture into mixing bowl and freeze solid. When ready to serve, remove bowl from freezer and allow mixture to soften just enough so that it can be beaten with an electric mixer. Beat until creamy but still quite thick and frozen. Serve immediately.

꘡

R2

LEMON GELATIN

4 servings

1 envelope unflavored gelatin
½ cup cold water
⅓ cup sugar

⅛ teaspoon salt
1 cup boiling water
¼ cup lemon juice

Soften gelatin in cold water. Add sugar, salt and boiling water and stir until dissolved. Add lemon juice; stir well and pour into individual serving dishes or a 2-cup mold. Chill for several hours.

For orange gelatin:

Use ¼ cup cold water, 1 tablespoon lemon juice, ¼ cup sugar along with gelatin, salt, boiling water and ½ cup orange juice; follow directions above.

꘡

R2

FRUIT GELATINS

4 servings

With natural ingredients, it is possible to make almost any fruit-flavored gelatin.

1 tablespoon unflavored
   gelatin
¼ cup cold water
¾ cup boiling water

1 cup fruit juice
Sugar
¼ teaspoon salt

Soak the gelatin in the cold water to soften. Dissolve in boiling water, stirring. Add 1 cup of the following fruit juices: orange, apricot, grapefruit, cranberry, grape, canned or cooked pineapple,* peach, etc. Stir in salt. If not sweet enough, add sugar to taste. Chill until mixture is set in mold which has been rinsed in cold water.

If desired, diced fruit may be added after gelatin has become the consistency of unbeaten egg whites.

NOTE: Sherry and other wines can be used for some or all of the fruit juice. Strong coffee can be substituted entirely to make coffee-flavored gelatin.

---

* Fresh pineapple juice contains an enzyme which prevents gelatin from setting.

II

APPETIZERS

F / R3
CAPONATA

2 medium eggplants
½ to ¾ cup olive oil
1 cup chopped celery
2 medium onions, chopped
1 cup coarsely chopped
   tomatoes

¼ cup capers, drained
¼ cup wine vinegar
1 tablespoon sugar
1 tablespoon pignoli (pine nuts)
Freshly ground black pepper to
   taste

Peel eggplant and cut into ¾-inch cubes. Heat oil in large skillet and cook eggplant in it over high heat until it is lightly browned, about 10 minutes. Stir often. Remove eggplant with slotted spoon. Place celery and onion in remaining oil in skillet; lower heat and cook until celery is tender. Add tomatoes, cover and continue to cook for 10 minutes longer, stirring occasionally. Add eggplant, capers, vinegar, sugar, nuts and pepper to taste and simmer over low heat for 5 minutes. Chill and serve cold with black bread.

Freeze, if desired.

R1
CHICKEN LIVER PÂTÉ IN ASPIC

Makes 5 cups

1 cup plus 2 tablespoons
   chicken broth
2 envelopes unflavored gelatin
3 tablespoons chopped green
   onion
½ cup Madeira or medium-dry
   sherry
3 tablespoons chicken fat

1 pound chicken livers
¼ cup chopped green onion
Salt and freshly ground black
   pepper to taste
¼ teaspoon nutmeg
½ teaspoon anchovy paste
   (optional)
Watercress for garnish

Sprinkle gelatin on chicken broth to soften. Cook over low heat, stirring, until gelatin is completely dissolved. Remove from heat and stir in ¼ cup Madeira and 3 tablespoons green onion.

Pour into 6-cup mold and chill until firm.

Meanwhile, sauté the livers and green onions in chicken fat until livers are tender and pink. Blend livers in blender with remaining Madeira until smooth. Add salt, pepper, nutmeg and anchovy paste; blend thoroughly. Spoon mixture in mold; cover and refrigerate overnight, or until firm. Unmold onto plate, garnish with watercress and serve with crackers.

R3

CLAM AND CHUTNEY DIP

Makes approximately 3 cups

1 pint sour cream
2 tablespoons chopped
    chutney
Few dashes hot pepper sauce

¼ teaspoon or more Curry
    Powder (page 39)
1 (7-ounce) can minced clams,
    drained

Combine all ingredients and mix well. Chill. Serve with crackers or raw vegetables.

R3

CURRIED CHEDDAR SNACKS

64 pieces

1 cup chopped black olives
½ cup chopped green onion
1½ cups shredded Cheddar
    cheese
½ cup Mayonnaise (page 42)

1 teaspoon or more Curry
    Powder (page 39)
Salt to taste
64 squares thinly sliced dark
    bread

Combine all of ingredients except bread. Refrigerate, if desired. To serve, spread on bread and broil until cheese melts.

F / R2

CURRIED MUSHROOM STRUDELS

Approximately 60

1 pound fresh mushrooms, finely chopped
¼ cup butter
1 teaspoon Curry Powder (page 39)
2 tablespoons lemon juice

½ cup sour cream
1 teaspoon salt
Freshly ground black pepper
½ cup additional melted butter
½ pound *phyllo*

Sauté mushrooms in butter with curry and lemon juice. Stir in sour cream, salt, pepper. Cool mixture and prepare *phyllo*. Keep *phyllo* covered with wax paper and damp towel while working with it. Cut each sheet into strips 3 inches wide. Working quickly, brush a strip with melted butter. Fold over ¼ inch of bottom edge. Put ½ teaspoon mushroom filling near folded edge and fold *phyllo* over filling so that bottom of dough meets side to form triangle, folding as you would

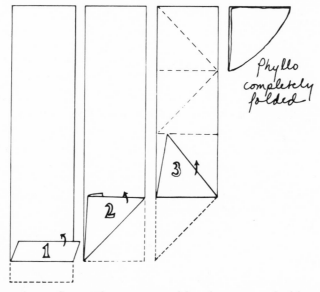

fold the American flag. Place seam side down on baking sheet. Brush tops with melted butter and bake at 400 degrees for about 15 minutes, until golden. Serve warm.

To make ahead, bake and freeze with layers of wax paper between triangles. To serve, defrost and bake at 350 degrees for about 15 minutes, until strudels are puffed and bubbly.

NOTE: *Phyllo*, paper-thin sheets of dough used extensively in Middle Eastern cooking, are best if purchased fresh but, if fresh ones are unavailable, they can be purchased frozen.

ℰ

R3 TO 4

GRAVLAX (MARINATED SALMON)

10 servings

Ulla Wachtmeister, wife of the Swedish Ambassador to the United States, sets one of the finest tables in Washington. She is an excellent cook and serves Swedish food. This is Countess Wachtmeister's recipe.

2 pounds center-cut fresh
  salmon
1 tablespoon sugar
1 tablespoon salt

1⅓ tablespoons coarsely ground
  black pepper
1 large bunch dill, coarsely cut
Mustard Sauce (below)

Split fish into 2 halves. Remove all the bones. Wash and wipe skin. Combine the sugar, salt and pepper and sprinkle over halves of flesh. Sprinkle on the dill and place two salmon halves flesh side together. Place in enamel or glass container and cover tightly. Place brick or other heavy weight on top of salmon and refrigerate for 3 to 4 days, turning salmon occasionally. Remove the dill and scrape off seasonings. Slice salmon thinly and garnish with fresh dill and lemon and serve with Mustard Sauce.

ℰ

MUSTARD SAUCE

2 tablespoons Dijon mustard
1 tablespoon sugar
2 tablespoons vinegar

6 tablespoons oil
1 heaping tablespoon chopped
  dill

Mix mustard with sugar and vinegar; add oil slowly, beating as you add. Stir in chopped dill and serve with Gravlax. Swedish mustard will make a much sweeter saucé.

᳙

HORSERADISH SAUCE

Enough for one recipe of Gravlax (page 66), or serve with smoked salmon.

3 heaping tablespoons prepared white horseradish with liquid thoroughly squeezed out
1 tablespoon powdered sugar

½ teaspoon dry mustard
2 tablespoons white wine vinegar
Salt and pepper to taste
1 cup heavy cream, whipped

Mix horseradish with sugar, mustard, vinegar, salt and pepper. Gradually add to whipped cream. Chill sauce for several hours before serving.

᳙

R3

HERB CHEESE

This is an inexpensive imitation of the French triple-cream Boursin.

2 large cloves garlic
8 ounces cream cheese (fresh, without gum if possible), softened
4 ounces farmer cheese

½ cup finely minced chives
½ cup finely minced parsley
Salt to taste
Freshly ground black pepper

Mash garlic; add with chives and parsley to cheeses. Beat well. Season with a little salt and a lot of pepper. Chill.

❧

R1

HERB-CHEESE STUFFED MUSHROOMS

Makes 36

This is the homemade version of mushrooms stuffed with the famous
French triple-cream cheese called Boursin.

36 medium-sized fresh mushrooms
8 ounces Herb Cheese (page 67)
Parsley

Remove the stems from the mushrooms by breaking off where they
join the cap. Rinse the caps and drain well to dry. Wipe with paper
towel, if necessary. Reserve stems for other use. Fill each mushroom
cap generously with the cheese. Refrigerate, if desired. To serve, decorate each stuffed mushroom with a small piece of parsley.

❧

F / R3

HERBED CHEDDAR CHEESE

Makes 1 cup

1 cup sharp Cheddar cheese, finely grated	½ teaspoon tarragon, rubbed fine
½ teaspoon sage	½ teaspoon chervil
½ teaspoon fennel seeds, crushed	1 tablespoon chopped fresh chives, or 1 teaspoon dried
½ teaspoon dill seeds, crushed	

Combine grated cheese with herbs and blend them in well. Place
mixture in 1-cup mold to shape, if desired. Refrigerate or freeze. To
serve, return to room temperature. Serve with bland crackers or raw
vegetables.

❧

R7

PIMIENTO CHEESE SPREAD

4-ounce jar pimientos, drained
½ pound grated sharp Cheddar
cheese

1 teaspoon dry mustard
2 tablespoons Mayonnaise
(page 42)

Chop drained pimientos and mix with cheese, mustard and mayonnaise until mixture is well mixed and moistened. Allow mixture to sit at room temperature for half an hour so flavors have a chance to blend.

Use as you would any cheese spread.

This will keep a week or longer in the refrigerator.

❧

HOT BRIE

1 large Brie, about 2¼ pounds
Slivered toasted almonds

Remove the center of the chalky white substance from the top of the Brie, leaving about an inch border and cutting about ⅛ inch or less deep.

Put Brie back into wooden box, which has been wrapped in heavy-duty aluminum foil.

Roast almonds at 400 degrees about 10 minutes, or until browned. Sprinkle toasted almonds in cutout section of Brie.

If you can put the cheese 8 to 10 inches from broiler, place Brie under broiler and heat until cheese becomes runny. But be careful it doesn't get too runny or it will fall apart. Watch carefully. Check after 8 to 10 minutes.

If you cannot get enough distance between heat and Brie, then put in 450-degree oven until Brie is runny.

Serve with unsalted crackers or French bread.

❧

F / R3

INDIAN CHEESE SPREAD

Makes 1¼ cups

This deliciously spicy recipe can be served with crackers or with raw vegetables as a dip.

2 tablespoons chutney
1½ to 2 teaspoons Curry Powder
  (page 39)
2 tablespoons English mustard

10 ounces finely grated sharp
  Cheddar cheese, at room
  temperature
4 tablespoons milk
2 tablespoons lemon juice

Cut chutney up finely and mix with curry. Work in remaining ingredients and chill before serving.

❧

F / R3

LIPTAUER CHEESE

Makes 1½ cups

A Middle European dish, it was originally made with Liptauer, a goat's milk pot cheese.

4 ounces pot cheese or small-curd
  dry cottage cheese
4 ounces cream cheese, softened
4 ounces butter, softened (1 stick)
1 tablespoon grated onion

½ teaspoon caraway seeds
1 teaspoon anchovy paste
1 teaspoon Dijon mustard
1 teaspoon paprika

Combine all ingredients and blend thoroughly. Freeze, or refrigerate up to a week. To serve, bring to room temperature and blend until quite smooth. Serve with black bread.

ॐ

R1

MARINATED TOMATOES AND OLIVES

Makes 4 cups

1 cup salad oil	1 bay leaf
1 cup cider vinegar	1 medium clove garlic, minced
2 teaspoons salt	1 pint cherry tomatoes
2 teaspoons sugar	2 (16-ounce) cans pitted ripe
1 teaspoon freshly ground black pepper	olives, drained

Mix together first 7 ingredients and beat well. With fork, pierce each tomato once; add to marinade. Add well-drained olives. Cover and refrigerate, stirring occasionally. To serve, remove tomatoes and olives with slotted spoon from marinade. Serve with cocktail picks.

NOTE: The liquid can be used again as a marinade or salad dressing.

ॐ

R1

MUSHROOMS STUFFED WITH MUSHROOMS

3 to 3½ dozen

½ pound fresh mushrooms, finely chopped *	1 cup light cream
¼ cup butter	2 teaspoons minced chives
3 tablespoons flour	1 teaspoon lemon juice
¾ teaspoon salt	36 to 42 large mushrooms, cleaned and stems removed

* Stems from the large mushrooms can be used as part of the ½ pound of finely chopped mushrooms.

Sauté chopped mushrooms in butter; blend in flour and salt. Stir in cream and cook until thick. Add chives and lemon juice. Cool. Stuff large mushroom caps with mixture. Heat mushrooms at 400 degrees for about 12 to 15 minutes, until filling begins to bubble and mushrooms begin to soften.

🐗

R1

MUSSELS À LA VIVAROIS

48 mussels; enough for
8 servings as first course;
about 16 as hors d'oeuvres

Adapted from the three-star Parisian restaurant Vivarois

4 dozen mussels, thoroughly
  cleaned
2 medium onions, minced
4 teaspoons peppercorns

4 sprigs parsley
1 teaspoon thyme
3 cups white wine
Garlic-Butter Mixture (page 73)

In advance, clean mussels thoroughly by scrubbing with a stiff brush and rinsing several times in cold water. Combine the next five ingredients in large pot with cover and cook over medium heat for 5 minutes.

Add the mussels; cover and cook for about 10 minutes, until mussels open. Remove mussels from liquid and leave mussels on one half-shell. Place a generous dab of Garlic-Butter Mixture in each mussel. Refrigerate, if desired. To serve, bake at 400 degrees for 10 minutes, until butter mixture is bubbly.

ᖱ

F / R3

GARLIC-BUTTER MIXTURE

¾ cup butter, creamed
6 tablespoons finely minced
   shallots
3 cloves garlic, crushed
6 tablespoons minced parsley

4 anchovy fillets, pounded to a
   paste
4 teaspoons anisette
2 teaspoons lemon juice

Combine creamed butter with remaining ingredients and blend thoroughly.

This mixture can be used with snails, too.

ᖱ

R1

MUSSELS RAVIGOTE

16 as hors d'oeuvres; 8 as first course

50 mussels, thoroughly scrubbed
   and soaked in cold water
½ cup dry white wine
1 **shallot, halved**

1 sprig parsley
4 peppercorns
Parsley for garnish

Sauce:

2 small shallots
2 tablespoons wine vinegar
2 tablespoons white wine
1½ teaspoons finely minced fresh
   tarragon, or ½ teaspoon
   dried
¾ cup mayonnaise
1½ teaspoons drained capers

1½ teaspoons finely minced
   parsley
1½ teaspoons finely minced
   chives
Freshly ground black pepper
   1 teaspoon Dijon mustard
Salt, if necessary

Combine the mussels, wine, shallot, parsley and peppercorns in heavy pot. Cover and cook until mussels open, 10 to 15 minutes. Discard any mussels that do not open. When they are cool enough to handle, open mussels and discard one shell half. Loosen mussels from remaining half and put back on half.

While mussels are cooking, combine shallots, vinegar, wine and tarragon in small pot. Cook over high heat until liquid evaporates completely. Combine this mixture with remaining sauce ingredients. Adjust seasoning, adding salt if necessary. Decorate mussels with a dab of mayonnaise mixture and a sprig of parsley and refrigerate until serving time. Serve cold.

F / R1

NACHOS

Approximately 8 dozen pieces

From the Land of Tex-Mex

1 dozen corn tortillas (if frozen, defrost)
Oil for frying

8 ounces Cheddar cheese, sliced (approximately)
1 (3-ounce) can jalapeño peppers

Cut each tortilla into 8 wedge-shaped pieces. Fry in hot oil until lightly golden. Cut wedge-shape pieces of cheese just a little narrower than tortilla wedges and place on top of tortillas. Place thin slivers of jalapeños on top of wedges. Freeze, if desired. To serve, defrost and place under broiler until cheese melts. Serve hot.

ᵥᵥ

F / R2

1, 2, 3 HORS D'OEUVRES

Approximately 70 pieces,
between the size of a quarter
and a half-dollar

A favorite from Betty Talmadge of Georgia

1 pound combination of hot and mild bulk pork sausage, or all hot
2 cups finely grated sharp Cheddar cheese
3 cups Biscuit Mix (page 53)

Combine sausage, cheese and Biscuit Mix; roll into balls the size of a marble. Freeze or refrigerate, if desired. To serve, bring to room temperature and bake in shallow pan at 350 degrees for 15 to 20 minutes, until golden brown on bottom.

ᵥᵥ

R3

POOR MAN'S CAVIAR

Makes approximately 4 cups

A Russian zakuska, or hors d'oeuvre

2 large eggplants
2 tablespoons olive oil
2 large onions, chopped fine
2 cloves garlic, minced
2 medium green peppers, chopped fine

2 (6-ounce) cans tomato paste
2 teaspoons white vinegar
Salt and freshly ground pepper to taste

Bake eggplants whole at 425 degrees on rack in center of oven for about one hour, turning a couple of times until soft and skin is charred and blistered. Remove skin from eggplant and chop meat fine. Heat 2 tablespoons of oil and cook onions, garlic and green pepper in oil until soft but not brown. Add tomato paste and simmer for 3 to 5 minutes. Stir in vinegar, salt and pepper and chopped eggplant and cook slowly for 30 minutes in skillet. Cool and serve thoroughly chilled as appetizer with thin slices of pumpernickel.

ॐ

R2

ROQUEFORT CHEESE MOLD

3-cup mold

1 package unflavored gelatin	Salt to taste
½ cup dry white wine	1½ teaspoons vinegar
1 cup boiling water	4 ounces Roquefort cheese,
2 tablespoons sugar	crumbled
2 tablespoons lemon juice	½ cup broken walnut meats
½ cup sour cream	Watercress or cherry tomatoes for
1 tablespoon minced parsley	garnish
½ teaspoon Worcestershire sauce	

Soften gelatin in wine. Dissolve in boiling water with sugar and lemon juice. Blend in sour cream, parsley, Worcestershire, salt and vinegar. Chill until mixture is syrupy. Stir in crumbled cheese and nuts. Turn into 3-cup mold and chill until firm. Unmold to serve. Fill center with watercress or cherry tomatoes; place crackers around the outside of mold.

❧

F / R1

SEAFOOD-STUFFED *PHYLLO*

30 to 35 pastries

1 tablespoon butter	1 cup crab meat or cooked
1 tablespoon flour	shrimp
½ cup milk	1 beaten egg yolk
Salt to taste	1 teaspoon lemon juice
3 shallots, finely chopped	Nutmeg and white pepper
1½ tablespoons butter	5 sheets 12-inch-wide *phyllo*
	⅛ to ¼ pound butter, melted

Prepare a béchamel sauce: Melt 1 tablespoon butter. Remove from heat and stir in flour. Carefully stir in milk and cook, stirring, until smooth and thick. Season with salt.

Sauté shallots in 1½ tablespoons butter. Add crab meat. To the béchamel sauce, add the beaten yolk, lemon juice, nutmeg and white pepper to taste. Gently stir in crab-meat mixture. Cool.

Keep *phyllo* covered with wax paper and damp towel while working with it. Cut each sheet into strips 2 inches wide. Working quickly, brush a strip with melted butter. Fold over ¼ inch of bottom edge. Put a teaspoon of filling near folded edge and fold *phyllo* over filling so that bottom of dough meets side, to form triangle, folding as you would fold the American flag (page 65). Place seam side down on baking sheet. Brush tops with melted butter and bake at 400 degrees for about 15 minutes, until triangles are golden. Serve warm.

To make ahead, bake and freeze with layers of wax paper between triangles. To serve, defrost and bake at 350 degrees about 15 minutes, until *phyllo* are puffed and bubbly.

ೞ

R1

SNAIL-STUFFED MUSHROOMS

3 per person as appetizer or first course

⅔ cup soft butter
1½ teaspoons finely minced
   shallots
 2 large cloves garlic, crushed
1½ tablespoons minced parsley

½ teaspoon salt
Freshly ground black pepper
18 snails
18 large mushroom caps, cleaned

Cream together the butter, shallots, garlic, parsley, salt and a few grinds of black pepper. Drain and rinse the snails. Put a little of butter mixture into each mushroom cap. Place snail on top of butter mixture; top with a little more butter. Let stand out for 2 or 3 hours, or refrigerate overnight. Bake at 400 degrees for 15 minutes, until bubbly and hot.

ೞ

R3

SOUR CREAM HORSERADISH SAUCE

Makes 1 cup

2 tablespoons finely minced
   shallots or green onions
1 tablespoon chopped fresh dill

¾ cup sour cream
 2 tablespoons white horseradish
 1 tablespoon Mayonnaise
   (page 42)

Combine ingredients and mix well. Use with any kind of marinated fish, or add 1 can rinsed and well-drained tuna which has been broken up into fine pieces. Serve with dark bread, such as pumpernickel or rye.

❧

F / R2

TIROPETAS

150 pastries

A Greek specialty

½ pound feta cheese
1 pint large-curd cottage cheese
12 ounces cream cheese
3 eggs

2 tablespoons finely chopped parsley
Dash pepper
⅛ teaspoon nutmeg
¾ pound *phyllo*
1 cup butter, melted

With fork, cream together until smooth the feta, cottage cheese and cream cheese. Add the eggs, one at a time, beating until smooth. Mix in the parsley, pepper and nutmeg. Lay out *phyllo* one sheet at a time (keep remaining covered with damp cloth) and cut into strips 1¾ inches wide. Brush each strip with melted butter. Fold over bottom edge ¼ inch. Place less than a teaspoon of filling on that end of pastry strip and fold over one corner to make a triangle; continue folding pastry from side to side in the shape of a triangle (like folding the American flag; page 65). Place seam side down on baking sheet. Continue in this manner until each baking sheet is filled. Then brush tops of pastries with melted butter and bake at 375 degrees for 15 to 18 minutes, until golden brown. Repeat this operation until all filling is used.

Refrigerate or freeze, if desired. To serve, if frozen, place directly from freezer in oven at 350 degrees and bake for about 15 minutes, or until heated through and butter is bubbling. If refrigerated, bake at 350 degrees about 10 minutes.

❧

R2

WALNUT BOURBON PÂTÉ

Makes approximately 5 cups

¼ pound butter
1 small onion, coarsely
  chopped
1 pound chicken livers
1½ cups chicken broth
2 tablespoons dry sherry
½ teaspoon paprika
¼ teaspoon allspice
¼ teaspoon ginger

⅛ teaspoon hot pepper sauce
Salt to taste
1 clove garlic, crushed
½ cup bourbon
1 envelope unflavored gelatin
1 cup chopped walnuts
Parsley and cherry tomatoes
  for garnish

Melt butter and add onion and livers. Cook about 10 minutes, until onion softens and becomes translucent. Add ¾ cup broth, sherry and seasonings. Continue to cook 5 minutes longer. Remove from heat and add bourbon. Sprinkle gelatin over remaining ¾ cup broth. Dissolve by heating broth over low heat. Place chicken liver mixture in blender and blend until smooth. Add broth mixture and walnuts. Spoon mixture into 5- or 6-cup mold and chill overnight. To serve, unmold and garnish with parsley and cherry tomatoes. Serve with dark bread or crackers.

III

SOUPS

꒚

F / R2

AVOCADO CURRY SOUP

4 or 5 servings

1 tablespoon butter
1 to 2 teaspoons Curry Powder
(page 39)
12 ounces Chicken Stock or
broth (page 90)

1 cup light cream
1 slightly beaten egg yolk
Few dashes hot pepper sauce
1 medium-size avocado

Melt butter; stir in curry and add stock. Bring to boil; cover and simmer 10 minutes. Combine cream with yolk and gradually stir into soup, cooking over low heat. Remove from heat. Mash half of avocado and dice the other half; add both to soup. Refrigerate or freeze, if desired. To serve hot, reheat, stirring constantly. To serve cold, if frozen, defrost and beat vigorously to blend.

꒚

F / R3

BEEF AND BARLEY SOUP

Makes approximately 2½ quarts

2 cups canned tomatoes
¾ pound boneless chuck, cut
into 1½-inch cubes
Salt and pepper to taste
Celery tops from ½ bunch
2 sprigs parsley
¼ cup regular barley
1 cup tomato juice

½ pound green beans, tips cut
off, washed and cut in half
½ cup coarsely chopped
rutabaga
1½ cups coarsely chopped
cabbage
½ cup sliced carrots
½ cup sliced celery
½ cup thinly sliced onion

Drain the liquid from the tomatoes and reserve. Add enough water to liquid to make 1 quart. Place in large kettle with beef, salt and pepper to taste, celery tops and parsley. Cover and cook slowly for 1 hour. Add barley. Cook 1 hour longer. Remove and discard celery tops and parsley. Add tomato juice, reserved tomatoes and remaining ingredients. Bring to a boil. Reduce heat and cook about 45 minutes.

Serve immediately, refrigerate or freeze. To serve, reheat.

BERMUDA FISH CHOWDER

Eight to ten 2-cup servings

3 pounds rockfish or sea bass	1 (28-ounce) can tomatoes
2 pounds any other fish fillets	1 (8-ounce) can tomato sauce
1 teaspoon salt	2 tablespoons chopped parsley
1½ teaspoons dried leaf thyme	¾ teaspoon Worcestershire
½ teaspoon ground cloves	sauce
1 bay leaf	¼ teaspoon hot pepper sauce
¼ cup butter or margarine	¼ teaspoon Curry Powder
2 onions, chopped	(page 39)
6 ribs celery, chopped	Lemon wedges
1 green pepper, chopped	Dark rum and sherry

Remove heads and tails of rockfish or sea bass. Discard tails. Place heads, fish bodies and fillets in large kettle. Add water just to cover, salt, thyme, cloves and bay leaf. Cover and simmer 15 minutes. Strain, reserving stock. Discard heads; remove skin and bone from fish and flake the fish. In large kettle melt butter; add onions, celery and green pepper. Cook until tender. Add tomatoes, tomato sauce, parsley, Worcestershire sauce, hot pepper sauce and curry powder. Simmer, uncovered, for 15 minutes. Add reserved fish stock and flaked fish. Simmer 15 minutes. Serve in heated soup bowls, adding a squeeze of lemon juice, a dash or two each of rum and sherry and additional hot pepper sauce to taste to each serving. Serve with warm crusty bread and butter.

❧

Rl

BLOODY MARY SOUP

6 servings

1 medium onion, sliced
3 stalks celery, diced
2 tablespoons butter
2 tablespoons tomato puree
5 cups tomato juice

2 teaspoons Worcestershire
  sauce
Salt and pepper to taste
1 tablespoon lemon juice
½ cup vodka

Sauté onion and celery in butter until golden. Add puree. Cook 1 minute. Add tomato juice and simmer 10 minutes. Add remaining ingredients; cook 1 minute longer; strain. Return to heat; bring to boil. Refrigerate at least 4 hours, or overnight. Serve ice-cold.

❧

Rl

BLUEBERRY SOUP

Makes approximately 5 cups

Fruit soups come from Scandinavia. They are served at the end of a meal, but they can be served at the beginning, too. They are not too sweet and, with a dollop of sour cream on top, become both tart and sweet. Peaches, sweet or sour cherries, and plums all make good fruit soups. If you use sweet cherries, you can substitute port wine for the vermouth. Incidentally, the port wine goes well with the blueberries, too.

1 pound fresh blueberries
  (1 pint), washed and drained
4 cups water
Peel of 1 lemon
½ cup dry vermouth

1 stick cinnamon
6 to 8 tablespoons sugar
3 cloves, whole
¼ cup fresh orange juice
1 cup sour cream

Place all ingredients, except the sour cream, in a saucepan and cook over medium heat until mixture begins to boil and berries begin to burst and turn soft. Remove cloves, lemon peel and cinnamon. Puree mixture, about 1 cup at a time, in blender. Chill thoroughly, preferably overnight, and serve with dollops of sour cream.

NOTE: To serve for dessert, top with dollops of whipped cream, accompanied by thin butter cookies.

༄

CLAM AND OYSTER BROTH

Makes 5 cups

1 pint oysters	¼ teaspoon celery seed
2 pints clams	Salt and pepper to taste
5 cups water	4 tablespoons butter
1 teaspoon Worcestershire sauce	

Drain the liquor from the oysters; reserve. Combine the clams with their liquor, the oyster liquor, water, Worcestershire sauce, celery seed and salt and pepper to taste. Bring to a boil. Sauté oysters in butter just until edges curl. Do not overcook. Just before serving, drop sautéed oysters in broth.

༄

R1

COLD SPINACH SOUP

8 servings

2 (10-ounce) packages fresh spinach, washed and tough stems removed	2 cups Chicken Stock (page 90)
	¼ cup dry vermouth
	1 teaspoon grated lemon rind
½ cup freshly minced onion	½ teaspoon mace
2 cups light cream	2 hard-cooked eggs, chopped

Cook the spinach in its own moisture with the onion until spinach is tender, about 3 to 5 minutes. Place in blender with some of the light cream and blend until smooth. Place the rest of the cream and the stock with the blended spinach in a pot and cook just until flavors are blended. Stir in vermouth, lemon rind and mace and chill thoroughly. Serve topped with chopped eggs.

❦

R2

IRANIAN CUCUMBER SOUP

6 servings

The yogurt base makes this Middle Eastern dish an extremely refreshing soup.

3 cups plain yogurt	¾ cup finely chopped walnuts
1½ cups grated cucumber	1 clove garlic, minced
½ cup seedless raisins	½ teaspoon salt
¾ cup cold water	¼ teaspoon white pepper
1 tablespoon minced fresh dill	

Beat yogurt in electric mixer or with rotary beater. Add cucumber and raisins. Blend in cold water. Add the remaining ingredients; blend well and chill thoroughly. Serve.

❦

R1

MO'S CLAM CHOWDER

12 to 14 very generous servings

1 pound nitrite-free bacon, diced	6 cups minced clams, drained
¼ pound nitrite-free smoked ham, diced	6 cups milk
	Salt and freshly ground black pepper to taste
6 cups chopped onion	Butter
¼ cup flour	Paprika
12 cups diced potatoes	

Sauté the bacon and ham until bacon is brown. Drain off the fat. Add the onion and sauté until it is limp. Stir in the flour. Add the potatoes and clams and cook about 15 minutes, until potatoes are very soft. Add the milk and season to taste with salt and pepper.

Serve hot with a dollop of butter and a sprinkling of paprika on top of each serving.

Can be reheated.

❧

R1

SHERLEY'S VICHY-SQUASH

4 servings

Since the first cookbook, my dear friend and longtime cooking companion, Sherley Koteen, has always had a recipe in each one.

1 zucchini, the size of a large cucumber	3 tablespoons finely chopped onion
2 tablespoons snipped fresh dill, or 2 teaspoons dried dill	1 small garlic clove, chopped
10 sprigs watercress, including stems	¾ to 1 teaspoon Curry Powder (page 39)
3 ounces cream cheese	2 teaspoons lemon juice
1 cup low-fat milk	¼ teaspoon ginger
1 tablespoon olive oil	Salt and pepper to taste

Combine all ingredients in blender and blend until mixture is smooth. Chill thoroughly and serve ice-cold, garnished with sprigs of watercress.

❦

R1

STRACIATELLI

6 servings

3 large eggs
4 heaping tablespoons freshly
grated Parmesan cheese

2 tablespoons finely minced
parsley
6 cups Chicken Stock (page 90)

Beat eggs until frothy. Stir in cheese and parsley. The egg mixture can be combined the day before. The soup stock can be made well ahead and frozen.

Bring broth to rolling boil. Pour beaten-egg mixture slowly into soup, stirring constantly until egg sets. Serve hot.

❦

F / R2

BEEF STOCK

Makes 8 or more cups of stock

3 pounds beef flanken
1 pound shinbone
1 knuckle
8 cups water

3 carrots, scraped and halved
1 onion, quartered
2 ribs celery, cut in half
Salt and pepper to taste

Place the beef plus shinbone and knuckle in pot with water. Bring to boil over medium heat. Skim off surface scum just before water boils. Add remaining ingredients; bring to boil again. Cover and lower heat so liquid simmers. Simmer for 2½ to 3 hours, until meat is so tender it almost falls apart. Strain stock. Cool stock and remove fat.

Freeze whatever stock is not used immediately in portions suitable for use in other recipes.

NOTE: Beef is delicious served cold with Horseradish Sauce (page 67).

❧

F / R2

CHICKEN STOCK

Makes 7 cups of stock

5 pounds chicken, cut up
2 quarts water
3 carrots, scraped and halved
1 onion, quartered

2 ribs celery, cut in half
1 tablespoon salt
½ teaspoon pepper

Combine ingredients in a large pot, cover and bring to boil. Reduce heat to simmer and cook for 30 to 40 minutes, until chicken is just tender. Strain stock. Cool stock and remove fat. Freeze whatever stock is not used immediately.

Use cold chicken for salads or casseroles.

❧

F / R3

FISH STOCK

Makes 3 quarts

3 pounds fish bones, heads and
  trimmings
4 quarts water
3 small bay leaves
8 peppercorns
1 teaspoon dried thyme

2 onions, chopped coarsely
2 carrots, scraped and chopped
  coarsely
2 celery stalks with leaves
Salt to taste

Wash the fish well. Place in pot with water and remaining ingredients. Bring to a boil and simmer 30 minutes. Strain. Refrigerate or freeze and use as needed.

Dry white wine may be added, from ½ cup to 2 cups, and cooked with the rest of the ingredients.

❧ IV ❧

POULTRY

⚬

R1

BARBECUED HONEY CHICKEN

4 servings

½ cup dry sherry	1 small clove garlic, crushed
2½ teaspoons cinnamon	Salt and pepper to taste
⅓ cup honey	3- to 3½-pound chicken,
2 tablespoons lime juice	cut in serving pieces

Mix together sherry, cinnamon, honey, lime juice, garlic and salt and pepper. Pour this mixture over chicken, turning pieces to coat well. Refrigerate overnight, or longer if desired. Remove and broil chicken over charcoal, basting with marinade, turning frequently.

⚬

R1

CARRIE LEE NELSON'S PEKING CHICKEN

4 servings

Mrs. Gaylord Nelson is the wife of the Wisconsin Senator. She is one of the finest non-Chinese Chinese cooks. This recipe is much like Peking duck, but a lot less expensive.

1½ tablespoons Chinese peppercorns	3 slices fresh ginger, cut ⅓ inch thick
1½ tablespoons salt	1 tablespoon star anise
1 (3½-pound) frying chicken	3 tablespoons flour
½ cup light Chinese soy sauce, or Japanese soy sauce	3 tablespoons black tea
2 tablespoons dry sherry	3 tablespoons brown sugar
5 cups water	8 *moo shi* wraplings (doilies)
2 green onions, cut in 2-inch sections	8 green onion "brushes"
	Hoisin sauce

Combine the peppercorns and salt. Fry over low heat in frying pan until salt is brown and peppercorns are dark and have taken on a distinctive aroma. Rub this mixture inside and outside of chicken and place in refrigerator overnight.

Combine soy sauce, sherry, water, green onions, ginger and star anise. Bring to boil; place chicken in boiling mixture and turn heat to medium. Cover and cook chicken 10 minutes on one side; turn and cook 10 minutes on second side. Turn off heat and let chicken cool in sauce with cover on for 20 minutes.

When ready to serve, prepare bed of charcoal in grill. Charcoal is ready when gray ash has formed on coals. Make a tray out of aluminum foil. Combine flour, black tea and brown sugar and sprinkle on tray. Place tray directly on charcoal. Place grill racks over charcoal and put chicken on rack. Cover grill with hood; be sure all vents are closed. Smoke chicken for 20 minutes. Chicken should be well browned.

Serve warm or cold, but not hot. Remove chicken from bone, but leave skin intact in large pieces. Serve pieces with wraplings which have been steamed to warm, accompanied by "brushes" and hoisin sauce.

The brushes are made by cutting the green from the white of the scallion. With knife, cut off root from white part of scallion, then slash end lengthwise to make brushlike appearance.

Each wrapling is spread with hoisin sauce, then a piece of chicken and scallion brush are enclosed in it. It is eaten with the fingers.

NOTE: To make this dish, a source of Chinese groceries is necessary.

ᴖᴗ

R1

CHICKEN IN RUM

3 or 4 servings

This recipe is adapted from one that is sold by Joyce Berthould in a farmers' market in Bethesda, Maryland.

Salt and pepper to taste
2 teaspoons Worcestershire
   sauce
1 tablespoon soy sauce
¼ cup Jamaican golden rum
2 cloves garlic, minced
½ cup minced chives

1 (3½- to 4-pound) chicken,
   cut in small pieces
4 tablespoons vegetable oil
3 tablespoons brown sugar
1 cup minced onion
¼ pound mushrooms, sliced
½ cup water
2 pimientos, sliced

Combine salt, pepper, Worcestershire, soy sauce, rum, garlic and chives to make a marinade. Marinate chicken in mixture for 4 or 5 hours, or overnight. Remove chicken from marinade and reserve the liquid.

Heat oil in heavy skillet. When it is very hot, add brown sugar. When sugar has melted and turned dark brown, add chicken. Cook 8 minutes, turning chicken occasionally until it has browned. Add onion and marinade; cook 5 minutes over high heat. Add mushrooms and ½ cup water; cover. Cook over medium to low heat for 30 minutes. Decorate with pimientos.

ও

F / R2

CHICKEN PROVENÇAL

4 servings

2 large cloves garlic,
   minced
2 anchovy fillets
1 (2-pound, 3-ounce)
   can tomatoes, well drained
¼ cup dry white wine
½ teaspoon dried thyme
½ teaspoon dried marjoram

1¼ teaspoons dried basil
Salt and pepper
1 (3- to 3½-pound) chicken,
   cut in serving pieces
Lemon juice
Flour
¼ cup olive oil
¾ cup chopped black olives

Combine garlic, anchovies, tomatoes, wine and seasonings together in a saucepan and cook over low heat for 1 hour, until thickened.

Brush skin of chicken with lemon juice and dust with flour which has been seasoned with salt and pepper. Brown on both sides in olive oil. Arrange chicken pieces in bottom of shallow casserole. Pour tomato sauce over the chicken. Sprinkle chopped olives on top. Refrigerate or freeze, if desired. To serve, return to room temperature and bake at 350 degrees for 40 to 50 minutes.

❧

R1

CHICKEN, ROMAN STYLE

4 servings

5 pounds chicken, cut in serving pieces
1/4 cup flour
2 teaspoons salt
1/2 teaspoon freshly ground black pepper
6 tablespoons or more butter
1/2 cup finely chopped onion
1/4 cup nitrite-free ham, cut in julienne strips

1/2 cup dry white wine
1/4 teaspoon dried rosemary
1 1/2 cups fresh or canned tomatoes, well drained
2 green peppers, sliced
2 medium cloves garlic, minced
2 tablespoons olive oil

Rub chicken pieces with mixture of flour, salt and pepper. Melt 4 tablespoons butter in skillet and brown chicken in it. Use more butter, if needed. Remove chicken. Melt 2 tablespoons butter and sauté onion and ham for 5 minutes. Return chicken to skillet and add wine and rosemary; cook over low heat until wine is absorbed. Add tomatoes. Cover and bake at 350 degrees for about 1 hour, or until chicken is done.

Meanwhile, sauté green pepper and garlic in hot olive oil. Fifteen minutes before chicken is done, add to chicken. Taste for seasoning and serve.

If desired, dish can be prepared to the point just before baking, and refrigerated. When you are ready to serve it, return it to room temperature and continue with directions.

ᴇ

CHICKEN WITH EGGPLANT

6 servings

8 cups eggplant, peeled and cut
  in shoestring strips
1 pound uncooked white chicken
  meat, cut in shoestring strips
2 tablespoons cornstarch
4 tablespoons dark Chinese soy
  sauce, or Japanese soy sauce
2 tablespoons dry sherry

½ cup peanut oil
10 dried hot red peppers (or
  fewer), finely chopped
2 cloves garlic, minced
2 tablespoons finely chopped
  fresh ginger
Salt to taste
1 cup Chicken Stock (page 90)

Cover eggplant with boiling water; let stand 5 minutes; drain well. Dredge the chicken meat in a mixture of cornstarch, soy sauce and sherry.

In large skillet or wok heat the oil; sauté the peppers until they take on a brownish-red color. Remove them from the pan. In the same pan sauté the chicken for about 2 minutes, until it is done. Add the eggplant, garlic, sautéed peppers, ginger, salt and chicken stock. Heat through and serve.

NOTE: When working with hot peppers, discard the seeds; they are the hottest part of the pepper. Do not touch your face with your hands while you are preparing the peppers as they are likely to cause a burning sensation. Wash your hands thoroughly with soap and water after working with the peppers.

ᴇ

ʀ1

CHINESE BARBECUED CHICKEN

4 servings

Remember Alice from the song "Alice's Restaurant"? This is a recipe adapted from one of Alice's.

Marinade:

1 cup light Chinese soy sauce, or
    Japanese soy sauce
1 cup dry sherry

2 large cloves garlic, minced
2 teaspoons fresh ginger, minced
4 pounds cut-up chicken

Sauce:

½ cup hoisin sauce
 1 cup dry sherry
½ cup catsup

¼ cup brown sugar
 1 clove garlic, minced

Combine marinade ingredients and pour over chicken pieces in shallow pan. Marinate overnight, turning occasionally if pieces are not completely covered. Combine sauce ingredients and set aside. To serve, remove chicken pieces from marinade. Place in shallow pan and cover with sauce. Bake at 350 degrees for 45 minutes, turning once, or until chicken is done. Baste several times.

CHINESE CHICKEN AND WALNUTS

8 to 10 servings

 6 tablespoons peanut oil
 2 cups bamboo shoots, cut in
    julienne strips
 4 cups Chinese cabbage, cut in
    julienne strips
 2 cups celery, cut in julienne
    strips
 2 cups onions, cut in julienne
    strips
16 water chestnuts, sliced
    paper-thin
 3 cups walnuts

1½ teaspoons salt
 4 tablespoons cornstarch
 2 teaspoons sugar
 4 tablespoons light Chinese soy
    sauce, or Japanese soy sauce
 4 tablespoons dry sherry
 3 pounds uncooked white meat
    of chicken, cut in julienne
    strips
 1 cup Chicken Stock or broth
    (page 90)

In a large skillet or wok heat 3 tablespoons of the oil. Lightly sauté bamboo shoots, cabbage, celery, onions and water chestnuts, cooking only until crisp-tender. Remove. Brown walnuts in same oil. Drain. Combine salt, cornstarch, sugar, soy sauce and sherry. Dredge chicken in this mixture. Heat remaining 3 tablespoons oil in skillet and quickly sauté the chicken in the hot oil until tender. Add the stock to the chicken; heat. Add the vegetables and nuts and heat through.

Serve with rice.

NOTE: For ease of preparation, have ready bamboo shoots, cabbage, celery, onions, water chestnuts and chicken. Combine salt, soy sauce, sherry, sugar and cornstarch; dredge chicken in it.

ツ

F / R2

MEXICAN CHICKEN

6 servings

2 (2½-pound) chickens, cut up
2 cups dry white wine
2 cups water
1 onion, cut in quarters
1 tablespoon salt
1½ cups tomato puree
1 cup sour cream
½ teaspoon *chile* powder
2 tablespoons finely chopped canned, or fresh, hot green *chiles*
½ to ¾ teaspoon cumin
½ teaspoon coriander
1 cup chopped onion
1 clove garlic, minced
8 ounces corn tortillas
Oil for frying
½ cup pitted ripe olives, halved
1¼ cups grated Cheddar cheese

Place chicken in large kettle with wine, water, onion and salt. Cover and simmer until meat is tender, about 45 minutes to 1 hour. Cool chicken, remove bones and skin and keep chicken in large pieces. Blend together tomato puree, sour cream, *chile* powder, green *chiles,* cumin, coriander, chopped onion, garlic. Cut each tortilla into 8 wedges and cook quickly in hot oil on both sides, until crisp, adding oil as needed. Drain thoroughly on paper. Layer chicken, sauce, tortillas, olives and cheese in 1½-quart casserole, reserving some cheese for top. Freeze, if desired. To serve, return to room temperature and bake at 350 degrees until hot and bubbly, about 25 to 30 minutes. Five minutes before finished, sprinkle on remaining cheese and cook until cheese melts.

ℰ

R1

STUFFED CHICKEN BREASTS

4 to 6 servings

3 whole chicken breasts, boned, skinned and halved
Salt and pepper to taste
6 thin slices nitrite-free country ham
¼ cup freshly grated Parmesan cheese

¾ cup chopped parsley
½ cup blanched slivered almonds
4 tablespoons butter
½ cup dry vermouth
2 tablespoons brandy
4 tablespoons Chicken Stock or broth (page 90)

Cut a pocket in each chicken breast very carefully. It doesn't need to be very big, but try not to have any tears or holes in it. Sprinkle with salt and pepper. Line pockets with ham. Combine cheese, parsley, and almonds and stuff each pocket with some of mixture. Heat butter in large skillet. Sauté breasts 8 to 10 minutes per side, or until golden. Start with pocket side down and cook slowly so very little stuffing comes out (some will). Turn carefully. Add vermouth and brandy. At this point dish may be refrigerated until serving time. To serve, cover skillet and bring liquid to boil; simmer gently for 10 to 15 minutes. Remove breasts to warm platter. Add stock to skillet; stir and heat through. Then pour liquid from skillet over chicken breasts and serve.

ℰ

ROAST GOOSE

If goose is frozen, thaw as you would a turkey (page 104). Remove excess fat from body cavity and neck skin. Fat may be rendered and used in other cooking. Rinse bird and drain. Salt cavity.

Fill neck and body cavity loosely with stuffing; or do not stuff, and put quartered onion and cut-up stalk of celery in cavity. Fasten neck skin back with skewer. Tie legs together or tuck in band of skin at tail, if present. Tie wings flat against body.

Place goose, breast side up, on rack in shallow roasting pan. Salt well. Prick all over with fork. If meat thermometer is used, insert deep into inside thigh muscle. Roast at 400 degreees for 45 minutes to 1 hour, depending on size of bird. During roasting, spoon off accumulated fat.

Reduce temperature to 325 degrees and continue roasting. Thermometer should reach 180 to 190 degrees. If thermometer is not used, press meaty part of leg between protected fingers. When bird is done, it should feel soft. Prick thigh with fork. Juices should run beige in color, not pink. Skin should be golden brown and crisp. See chart for roasting time.

Leftover stuffing should be removed from bird. Refrigerate separately from meat.

ROASTING TIMETABLE
(*STUFFED WHOLE GOOSE*)

READY-TO-COOK WEIGHT (POUNDS)	TIME AT 400 DEGREES F.	PLUS TIME AT 325 DEGREES F. (HOURS)	TOTAL ROASTING TIME (HOURS)
6 to 8	45 minutes	1 to 1½	1¾ to 2¼
8 to 10	1 hour	1¼ to 2	2¼ to 3
10 to 12	1 hour	2 to 2½	3 to 3½
12 to 14	1 hour	2½ to 2¾	3½ to 3¾

For unstuffed goose:

8-pound goose, deduct 20 minutes

9-pound goose, deduct 25 minutes

10-pound goose, deduct 30 minutes

ROAST TURKEY

Allow at least ¾ pound per serving for turkeys under 12 pounds. Allow ½ to ¾ pound for turkeys over 12 pounds.

Fresh turkeys should be washed, dried and allowed to come to room temperature before being stuffed and cooked. Stuffing should never be placed in bird until just before cooking. Turkeys should never be cooked overnight at a low temperature. In both cases the idea is to prevent spoilage, for bacteria will multiply rapidly under such conditions.

Frozen unstuffed turkeys may be brought to room temperature by two different methods. Thaw the bird in its wrapper on a tray in the refrigerator. Allow 1 to 2 days if under 12 pounds; 2 to 3 days if between 12 and 20 pounds; and up to 4 days if over 20 pounds.

To hasten the process, thaw a turkey under 12 pounds at room temperature for 6 hours and return to the refrigerator for 12 hours. Allow 8 hours out and 12 in for birds 12 to 18 pounds, and 10 hours plus 12 hours for those larger.

Generally, the stuffed and trussed bird is placed on the rack breast up. Oil or butter is rubbed over the skin of the bird, which is then basted every 20 minutes or so.

Aluminum foil may be used as a tent over the bird or applied in the later stages over breast and drumsticks to keep browned skin from burning.

Allow about ½ hour after the bird comes from the oven before carving. This allows the juices to "set," meaning moister meat, and carving becomes easier.

Times for roasting are indicated in the accompanying table.

TIMETABLE FOR ROASTING TURKEY

Internal Temperature 185 Degrees

READY-TO-COOK WEIGHT	APPROXIMATE TOTAL COOKING TIME
6 to 8 pounds	3 to 3½ hours
8 to 12 pounds	3½ to 4½ hours
12 to 16 pounds	4½ to 5½ hours
16 to 20 pounds	5½ to 6½ hours
20 to 26 pounds	6½ to 7 hours

This timetable is based on chilled or completely thawed turkeys at a temperature of about 40 degrees and placed in preheated (325 degrees) oven. For unstuffed turkeys reduce roasting time by 5 minutes per pound.

If a thermometer is not used, test for doneness about 30 minutes before timetable so indicates. Move drumstick up and down—if done, the joint should give readily or break. Or press drumstick meat between fingers; the meat should be very soft.

COOKING TURKEY IN FOIL

Prepare turkey as directed for roast turkey. To wrap, place turkey breast side up in middle of large sheet of heavy-duty aluminum foil. (For larger birds, join 2 widths of foil.)

Brush with shortening, oil or butter. Place small pieces of aluminum foil over the ends of legs, tail and wing tips to prevent puncture. Bring long ends of aluminum foil up over the breast of turkey and overlap 3 inches. Close open ends by folding up foil so drippings will not run into pan. Wrap loosely and do not seal airtight.

Place wrapped turkey breast up in open shallow roasting pan in oven at 450 degrees. Follow timetable for approximate time. Open foil once or twice during cooking to judge doneness. When thigh joint and breast meat begin to soften, fold back foil completely to brown turkey and crisp skin.

TIMETABLE FOR COOKING IN FOIL

Internal Temperature 185 Degrees

READY-TO-COOK WEIGHT	APPROXIMATE TOTAL COOKING TIME
7 to 9 pounds	2¼ to 2½ hours
10 to 13 pounds	2¾ to 3 hours
14 to 17 pounds	3½ to 4 hours
18 to 21 pounds	4½ to 5½ hours

ℰ

R1

PRUNE TURKEY STUFFING

Enough for 20- to 26-pound bird

1½ cups snipped pitted prunes	⅓ cup minced onion
⅔ cup orange juice	2 eggs, slightly beaten
½ cup melted butter	Salt and pepper to taste
8 cups toasted diced bread	Dash cayenne
1 cup peeled, diced apple	1 teaspoon ginger
⅔ cup minced celery	

Soak prunes in orange juice for 1 hour. Mix bread with remaining ingredients, including prunes. Refrigerate, if desired.

Stuff turkey lightly, allowing for expansion. Roast turkey as directed.

ℰ

R1

VICTORIAN STUFFED TURKEY

Enough for 10- to 13-pound turkey

1-pound loaf unsliced white bread	½ of 12-ounce can chestnuts, drained and broken in small pieces
½ of 1-pound loaf egg bread, unsliced	½ pound fresh sausage
¾ cup rye bread, torn in bits	Turkey liver, diced
¼ pound butter	Salt and pepper to taste
3 onions, finely chopped	Sage and thyme to taste
½ of large bunch of celery, including leaves, chopped	2 eggs
3 ounces fresh mushrooms, sliced	3½ to 4 cups Chicken Stock (page 90)
	1 pint oysters and liquid, optional

Cube bread in ½-inch cubes. Add rye. Place in large roasting pan in 275-degree oven and bake until dry, like Melba toast; turn often. Melt butter; add onions and celery. Cover and cook until onions are slightly golden. Add mushrooms and cook, covered, for 10 to 15 minutes.

Add onion mixture to bread with chestnuts. Fry sausage until brown; drain off fat, reserving a little of the fat in which to cook the turkey liver. Cook turkey liver. Add sausage to stuffing mixture. Add turkey liver. Season with salt, pepper, sage and thyme. Beat eggs well; add. Carefully stir in chicken broth. If oysters are used, poach them in their own liquor until edges curl; cut them in half and add to stuffing. Adjust seasoning and stuff turkey cavity and neck.

ੴ

HICKORY-SMOKED TURKEY

10 to 12 servings

Just as delicious as the very expensive kind you buy in the fancy delicatessen

10- to 12-pound ready-to-cook turkey Salt	½ pound butter, flavored with Seasoned Salt (page 38)

You will need an outdoor grill with a hood and a motor-driven spit.

Wash turkey and rub cavities with salt. Place turkey on the spit, putting spit in on the diagonal to keep turkey balanced. Skewer in place and then truss so that wings and other appendages do not fly around.

Have very slow coals in the back of the firebox, a drip pan under the bird as it revolves on the spit. Place a small pan of water at one end of the firebox for moisture.

Roast, hood down, basting every half-hour with butter mixture. Toss damp hickory chips on coals. Every 30 minutes or so, check the fire, adding water and hickory chips when they have disappeared. Empty the drip pan several times so fire cannot start from the collected grease.

Although most directions say to roast for 4½ to 5 hours, turkeys are often done in 3¼ to 3½ hours. Watch the bird carefully. The skin will turn black; this is natural.

Test turkey for doneness (see directions under Roast Turkey, page 105). Remove from spit and allow to sit for 30 minutes before carving.

Some people will like the burnt skin, others will not. Slice as you would any turkey and serve warm or cold.

V

FISH

❧

EGG FOO YONG

3 servings

6 eggs
2 cups bean sprouts, washed and drained
2 tablespoons finely chopped onion
1 teaspoon salt
Pepper to taste
1 cup crab meat, cooked shrimp or other fish

Salad oil
1 tablespoon sugar
1 tablespoon cornstarch
3 tablespoons light Chinese soy sauce, or Japanese soy sauce
1½ cups water

The batter can be made ahead. Beat eggs. Add bean sprouts, onion, salt, pepper and crab meat. Refrigerate, if desired. To serve, beat to mix again. Grease skillet with a little salad oil. Cook 6 separate pancakes on both sides until golden brown. Keep them warm as they are done.

Make a sauce as follows, preparing mixture ahead of time: Mix sugar and cornstarch. Add soy sauce and water. When ready to serve, cook mixture until thickened, stirring occasionally. Serve hot with hot pancakes.

❧

GRILLED ROCKFISH WITH FENNEL

6 servings

This is the American version of a famous Mediterranean dish, *loup de mer* with dried fennel. *Loup de mer* is unavailable here, and even a whole rockfish isn't easy to come by, although you can usually find fillets. Dried fennel is found in a few specialty shops, so . . .

1 whole rockfish (striped bass)
   weighing about 6 pounds, or 2
   bass fillets weighing 3 pounds
   each
1 tablespoon fennel seed

1 teaspoon salt
Freshly ground black pepper to
   taste
¼ cup olive oil
1 tablespoon brandy

Rinse the fish and dry on paper towels. If you are using a whole fish, have the head and tail removed and the inside cleaned. Cut 3 or 4 slashes in the skin of the whole fish or fillets, but not all the way through. Place the fillets together, sandwich-style.

Crush the fennel seeds either by placing them between 2 sheets of wax paper and using a rolling pin, or with a mortar and pestle. Combine the crushed fennel with the salt, pepper, oil and brandy.

Beat the mixture well and brush over the skin of the fish on both sides, being sure extra amounts are put in the slashes. Place the whole fish, or the fillets (laid together flesh to flesh), in a hinged grill and cook over medium charcoal fire about 5 inches from coals for about 8 minutes on each side, until the skin is crisp and well browned and flesh flakes easily with fork.

Remove fish from grill and remove bones from whole fish. Slice into 6 servings and serve with lemon wedges.

ᛘ

KOULIBIAC

10 servings

A glorious Russian dish

2 pounds fresh salmon
7 tablespoons butter
½ pound mushrooms, chopped
1 cup chopped onion
5 hard-cooked eggs, coarsely
   chopped
1½ cups cooked rice

5 tablespoons chopped fresh
   parsley
3 tablespoons chopped fresh
   dill weed
Salt and freshly ground black
   pepper
1 pint sour cream, optional

Cut salmon into thin slices and sauté in 4 tablespoons butter until cooked. Sauté mushrooms and onions in 3 tablespoons butter. Combine with eggs, rice, parsley and dill and mix well. Carefully mix in salmon. Season with salt and pepper. Chill until ready to make *koulibiac.*

Pastry for koulibiac:

4 cups unbleached flour
1 cup unsalted butter, chilled and cut in small pieces

2 tablespoons rum
¾ cup ice water, approximately
1 egg, beaten

Combine flour and butter and work in butter with fingertips until mixture resembles coarse cornmeal. Add rum with water and mix. Toss together. If dough is crumbly, add more water. Dough should be stiff. Divide dough in half and wrap well; refrigerate for several hours (it can be refrigerated for several days as well).

Place one ball of dough on floured board and roll into rectangle about ⅛ inch thick, brushing with more flour if needed. Trim into a rectangle about 10 x 17 inches. Place dough on greased cookie sheet and place filling on dough, leaving an inch border all the way around. Brush border with beaten egg. Roll remaining ball into rectangle 8 x 15 inches. Drape over rolling pin and place over filling. Seal bottom edges of pastry border over top, using fingers, and flute edges as for a pie.

Top can be decorated by rolling out remaining scraps cut into shapes. Brush top of pastry with beaten yolk; decorate with cutouts, if desired.

The *koulibiac* can be put together several hours ahead. Remove from refrigerator 1 hour before baking. Bake at 400 degrees for 30 minutes; reduce heat and bake at 350 degrees for 30 minutes longer, until golden brown. If pastry becomes too brown, cover lightly with aluminum foil while baking. Serve at once with sour cream, if desired.

If the *koulibiac* is to be baked as soon as it is assembled, refrigerate it for 20 minutes first.

❧

R1

MO'S SEAFOOD IN CHEESE SAUCE

8 to 10 servings

Mo runs the best seafood joint on the Oregon coast, in the town of Newport Beach.

½ cup butter	½ cup chopped black olives
½ cup flour	1½ teaspoons chopped pimiento
4 cups milk	1 pound cooked shrimp
2 teaspoons salt	1 pound crab meat
¼ pound mushrooms, sliced	2 teaspoons Worcestershire
1½ teaspoons chopped green	sauce
pepper	4 cups grated sharp Cheddar
⅓ cup chopped green onion	cheese

Melt the butter; stir in the flour. Off the heat, add the milk and stir to make smooth mixture. Return to heat and cook until smooth and thickened. Season with salt and add the mushrooms, green pepper, green onion, olives, pimiento and Worcestershire. Mix well. Stir in shrimp and crab and 3 cups of cheese. Cook over very low heat until cheese is melted. Turn into shallow casserole and sprinkle top with remaining cup of cheese.

Refrigerate, if desired, until serving time. To serve, bake at 350 degrees for 25 to 30 minutes, until the dish is heated through and cheese is melted.

ᔕ

MOULES MARINIÈRE

4 servings

With crusty bread and a salad, enough for a complete meal

4 pounds mussels	1 teaspoon thyme
2 medium onions, minced	3 cups white wine
4 teaspoons peppercorns	6 tablespoons butter
4 sprigs parsley	2 tablespoons minced parsley

Wash mussels in several changes of cold water, scrubbing thoroughly. In large pot with cover, combine onion, peppercorns, parsley sprigs, thyme and wine. Cook for 5 minutes. Add mussels; cover and cook 10 minutes, until shells open. Discard any which do not open. Keep mussels hot. Strain pan juices through fine sieve or triple layer of cheesecloth. Reduce pan liquid by half over high heat. Remove from heat; stir in butter and minced parsley. Pour over mussels and serve.

ᔕ

OVEN-TOASTED SHAD ROE

4 servings

1½ pounds shad roe	Pinch of cayenne
½ tablespoon prepared mustard	Pinch of rosemary
1 teaspoon anchovy paste	1 tablespoon butter
1 tablespoon Worcestershire sauce	3 tablespoons dry sherry
	3 drops bitters
	4 slices hot buttered toast
	1 lemon, sliced

Place roe in saucepan; cover with boiling water; reduce heat immediately and simmer roe gently for 15 minutes. Drain. Cut roe into

1-inch pieces. While roe is simmering, blend mustard, anchovy paste, Worcestershire, cayenne, rosemary, butter, sherry and bitters. When roe is done, dip drained pieces in mustard mixture until well coated; arrange on hot buttered toast and bake at 400 degrees for 5 minutes. Garnish with lemon slices.

REPUFFABLE SHRIMP OR TUNA SOUFFLÉ

4 to 6 servings

3 tablespoons butter	1 cup finely chopped cooked
2 tablespoons cornstarch	shrimp, or well-drained canned
½ teaspoon salt	tuna
¼ teaspoon pepper	4 egg yolks
1 cup milk	5 egg whites

Have ready a buttered 2-quart soufflé dish.

Melt butter over low heat. Remove from heat and blend in cornstarch and seasonings. Slowly stir in milk until mixture is smooth. Cook and stir over medium heat until sauce boils and thickens, 5 to 6 minutes. Add shrimp or tuna. Remove from heat. Cool for 5 minutes. Beat egg yolks well. Slowly stir a little of cooled shrimp mixture into yolks, beating vigorously. Return yolk mixture to shrimp mixture and mix well. Beat whites until stiff but not dry. Fold into shrimp base. Pour into soufflé dish and set in shallow pan containing an inch of hot water. Bake at 350 degrees for 1 to 1¼ hours.

To repuff, leave in soufflè dish; set dish in shallow pan with 1 inch of hot water. Reheat at 350 degrees until puffed, about 25 to 30 minutes.

NOTE: You can substitute 1 cup finely cut-up cooked chicken or turkey, cooked vegetables, ham or pork.

〜

R1

SALMON CUCUMBER SOUFFLÉ

8 to 10 servings

2 envelopes unflavored gelatin
½ cup cold water
½ cup Chicken Stock (page 90)
1 cup Mayonnaise (page 42)
2 teaspoons Worcestershire
 sauce
1 teaspoon salt
½ teaspoon pepper
2 tablespoons grated onion

2 tablespoons vinegar
2 pounds boneless salmon,
 cooked, or 2 (1-pound) cans red
 salmon, drained and flaked
3 cups peeled, diced cucumber
1 cup heavy cream, whipped stiff
3 egg whites, beaten stiff
Cucumber slices
French Dressing (page 45)

In large bowl sprinkle gelatin on cold water to soften. Heat stock to boiling; stir into softened gelatin until dissolved; cool. When cool, add mayonnaise, Worcestershire, salt, pepper, onion and vinegar, beating until smooth. Refrigerate, stirring occasionally, until mixture mounds when dropped from spoon.

Meanwhile, fold a 30-inch length of foil, 12 inches wide, in half lengthwise. Wrap around outside of a 2-quart soufflé dish so collar stands 3 inches above rim. Fasten with tape.

Beat mayonnaise mixture with eggbeater until light and fluffy. Fold in salmon, cucumber, whipped cream and beaten egg whites. Turn into prepared soufflé dish and refrigerate until firm.

To serve, remove foil collar; garnish with cucumber slices that have been marinated in French Dressing.

❦

SALMON IN PARCHMENT

4 servings

2 shallots, minced
8 mushrooms, sliced
2 tomatoes, peeled, seeded and
    diced
1 cup dry white wine

Salt and white pepper
4 (4 to 6 ounces) salmon or rock-
    fish fillets
1 cup heavy cream

Combine the shallots, mushrooms, tomatoes, wine, salt and pepper and spoon into shallow baking dish. Place salmon fillets on the mixture, cover and simmer on top of stove about 5 to 7 minutes, until the salmon is half done. Drain salmon thoroughly and remove to platter. Continue to drain liquid as it accumulates. Boil the sauce until there is almost no liquid left; add the cream and stir. Cook slowly for 1 hour, or until mixture is quite thick. It can be done ahead of time and sauce refrigerated, the salmon refrigerated separately.

Fold 4 sheets of parchment paper in half crosswise. Cut into heart shapes, as large as possible. Open and butter lightly. Place the thoroughly drained fish on one half of heart; top with sauce and fold other half of heart over. Seal by folding the two edges together all the way around to make a pleat. The point of the heart can be held in place with a straight pin. The recipe can be prepared up to an hour ahead at this point.

Bake at 400 degrees for 12 to 15 minutes. Serve fish in parchment.

❦

SALMON WITH SORREL

4 servings

From former White House chef René Verdon, who now owns Le Trianon Restaurant in San Francisco.

½ cup dry white wine
1 cup dry vermouth
2 shallots, minced
Few dashes lemon juice
Salt and freshly ground white
  pepper

32 leaves fresh sorrel, stems removed, steamed until limp
  and then shredded
6 (6-ounce) salmon or rockfish
  (striped bass) fillets
1 cup heavy cream

Combine wine, vermouth, shallots, lemon juice, salt, pepper and shredded sorrel. Place in shallow baking dish. Place fish fillets on top; cover and simmer on top of stove 10 to 15 minutes, until fish is cooked. Remove fish to platter; drain and keep warm. Boil liquid until it is reduced by half. Add cream and cook until mixture thickens. Serve over fish.

WHOLE GRILLED FISH

8 servings

12 slices nitrite-free bacon
10 sprigs parsley
Salt and white pepper to taste
1½ to 2 cups dry white wine

6 to 8 pounds whole fish (salmon,
  striped bass, etc.), slit, cleaned,
  head and tail removed after
  weighing

Lay 8 slices of bacon and the parsley inside the fish. Season inside and out with salt and pepper. Lay 4 slices of bacon on top of fish. Place fish on double thickness of heavy-duty aluminum foil with enough additional foil to make tight package. Shape foil so that it will hold the wine. Pour wine over fish. Secure package tightly and place 4 to 5 inches from medium hot coals. Cook for 45 minutes to 1 hour, or until fish flakes easily when tested. Remove foil, bacon and parsley. Remove bones and serve.

NOTE: Three pounds of salmon fillets (2 fillets put together) will cook in 30 minutes, using half of the other ingredients. Will serve 6.

❧ VI ❧

─────────────

MEATS

⛧

F / R2

ANISE BEEF

4 servings

Made with chuck beef, this is a very reasonably priced Chinese dish, but a lot of fat must be cut away; other cuts of braising beef will require less trimming.

2 pounds beef chuck	1 teaspoon salt
1 clove garlic	1 tablespoon dry sherry
2 tablespoons peanut oil	Dash pepper
3 tablespoons dark Chinese soy sauce, or Japanese soy sauce	2 cloves star anise *
1 tablespoon water	1 teaspoon sugar

Trim as much fat as possible from beef. Crush garlic. Heat oil in heavy pan; brown beef quickly on all sides. Add garlic, soy sauce, water, salt, sherry, pepper, star anise and sugar. Cover and simmer for 1 hour. Turn meat and simmer 1 hour longer. Cook longer, if necessary, until tender. Slice meat thinly and serve hot. If desired, refrigerate or freeze after slicing. To serve, return to room temperature; skim off excess fat and heat through at 350 degrees for 15 minutes.

⛧

R1

BEEF ROLL-UP

6 servings

1½ pounds ground beef	½ teaspoon caraway seeds
½ cup caraway rye bread crumbs	1 tablespoon Worcestershire sauce
1 egg	Salt and pepper to taste
½ cup chopped onion	1¾ cups sauerkraut, well drained
¼ cup sweet pickle relish	1½ cups grated Gruyère cheese
¼ cup Thousand Island Dressing (page 44)	

---

* If star anise is unobtainable, use anise extract, but only a few drops.

Combine meat, bread crumbs, egg, onion, and all seasonings in large bowl. Work mixture thoroughly with hands. On sheet of wax paper, shape the mixture into a rectangle about 7 x 15 inches. Sprinkle with sauerkraut and grated cheese, leaving a 1-inch border around all edges. Starting with narrow end, carefully roll up mixture, like a jelly roll. The wax paper acts as a guide only; don't roll up the paper inside the beef. Refrigerate, if desired. To serve, return to room temperature and place on shallow baking dish. Bake at 350 degrees for 30 to 45 minutes.

ぎ

F / R2

BRACIOLE

4 to 6 servings

These are Italian meat rolls.

1 tablespoon finely chopped parsley	2 hard-cooked eggs, quartered
1 teaspoon minced garlic	2 slices provolone cheese, cut into 4 strips each
1/4 teaspoon dried sage	Salt and pepper to taste
1 1/2 pounds beef bottom round	Olive oil
3/4 cup ground or finely chopped cooked beef and nitrite-free ham	1 1/2 cups chopped onion
	1 cup dry red wine
16 julienne strips of nitrite-free country ham	8 large fresh mushrooms, sliced
	3/4 cup tomato sauce

Combine parsley, garlic and sage. Cut the bottom round into 8 slices and pound flat (sometimes you can get the butcher to slice it for you, and then it is thin enough so that it doesn't have to be pounded). At the narrow end of each piece of beef, place 1 1/2 tablespoons ground meat, 2 pieces ham, 1/4 egg, 1 strip provolone, parsley mixture, salt and pepper to taste. Roll up and fold in sides. Secure with toothpick. Repeat until all meat is used.

Roll *braciole* in oil, salt and pepper. Pour a little oil into heavy skillet and brown *braciole* on all sides. Add the onion and brown. Add the wine and cook quicky over high heat. Add mushrooms and tomato sauce. Place meat and sauce in covered baking dish. At this point the dish can be refrigerated or frozen, if desired. To serve, return to room temperature and bake at 350 degrees for 45 to 60 minutes. If top rolls seem to be drying out, spoon sauce over and continue baking.

❧

R2

CHINESE POT ROAST

4 servings

2 (10-ounce) packages fresh
  spinach
2 tablespoons peanut oil
1 clove garlic
One 4- to 6-pound brisket of beef,
  trimmed of fat, or fresh picnic
  ham skinned and trimmed
  of fat

Pepper to taste
½ cup dry white wine
 2 cups light Chinese soy sauce,
  or Japanese soy sauce
½ cup sugar
 1 teaspoon Five Spice Powder
  (page 39)

Clean spinach and set aside. Heat oil in heavy pot; add garlic and meat. Brown meat on all sides. Pour off fat. Add pepper, white wine, soy sauce, sugar and spices and 4 cups water. Cover and bring to boil. Reduce heat and simmer for 2 to 3 hours, until meat is tender. When meat is cooked, remove from pot and slice. Arrange sliced meat on serving platter and keep warm.

Skim as much fat as possible from cooking liquid and place spinach in liquid in pot. Turn heat to high for 2 to 3 minutes and cook spinach, stirring constantly. Remove. Trim meat platter with spinach and serve.

❧

R3

CORNED BEEF

8 servings

1 (4-pound) beef brisket, fat
  removed
4 quarts hot water
1½ pounds salt, plus salt for
  coating

2 bay leaves
12 peppercorns
2 cloves garlic, cut in half
4 teaspoons Mixed Pickling
  Spice (page 46)

Wash and dry beef. Rub with 3 to 4 tablespoons salt. Dissolve 1½ pounds salt in hot water. Place beef in an enameled or glass pot or stone crock and pour salted water over it. Cool. Stir in a bay leaf, half the peppercorns, 1 clove garlic and half the pickling spices. Weight meat with plate, brick or other heavy object, if necessary, so that meat is completely covered with liquid. Cover pot. Allow to sit at room temperature for 48 hours. (Meat will not be pink, because it has no sodium nitrite in it.)

To cook, wash meat to remove brine. Place in pot with boiling water to cover, remaining peppercorns, garlic clove and pickling spice. Cover and simmer for 4 hours, or until fork-tender.

Serve as you would any corned beef, warm or cold, thinly sliced.

❧

F / R2

KESHY YENA

8 servings

Keshy Yena comes from the word in Spanish for cheese, *queso,* and the word for filled, *llena.* Spanish is one of the several languages that

go into making up the language spoken on the Dutch island of Curaçao
—Spanish, Dutch and English, with a smattering of Portuguese, French
and African. Originally, *Keshy Yena* was served in a scooped-out Edam
cheese, but the Edam is so expensive that, while the dish is not as
handsome this way, it is considerably less expensive. We've made some
of our own adjustments, too.

2 pounds round steak, cut into strips as thin as possible
¼ cup flour
Salt and freshly ground black pepper to taste
½ cup vegetable oil
½ cup dry red wine
2 green peppers, coarsely chopped
½ cup finely chopped onion
½ pound fresh mushrooms, sliced
2 medium tomatoes, coarsely chopped
¼ teaspoon cayenne pepper
1 tablespoon finely chopped sour pickle
3 tablespoons seedless raisins, or chopped prunes
6 small pimiento-stuffed olives, drained and finely chopped
1¼ cups Beef Stock (page 89)
1 pound Edam or Gouda cheese

Dredge beef strips in flour with salt and pepper. Heat ¼ cup oil in
heavy pan and cook beef strips in it until browned. Add the wine and
cook 1 or 2 minutes, then remove from heat and set aside.

Heat remaining oil and cook green peppers, onion and mushrooms
in it until soft but not brown. Add tomatoes and cayenne and cook
briskly until most of liquid in pan has evaporated. Remove from heat.
Stir in pickle, raisins or prunes, and olives. Combine vegetable mixture
with beef. Blend well and add beef stock.

Line a 3-quart casserole with round slices of cheese ⅛ inch thick.
Reserve some of cheese for top. Spoon mixture into casserole and top
with remaining cheese slices. Bake at 350 degrees for 20 to 30 minutes,
or until cheese is brown and bubbly.

If prepared ahead, refrigerate or freeze. To serve, return to room
temperature and bake as directed for 30 minutes.

ও

F / R2

PASTICHIO

6 to 8 servings

It is an interesting thing about this Greek dish—the natives serve it at
room temperature, but Americans prefer it hot.

Meat Sauce:

1 tablespoon butter	¼ teaspoon cinnamon
1 onion, finely chopped	½ cup dry white wine or beef
1 pound lean ground beef	stock
1 teaspoon salt	¾ cup tomato sauce
¼ teaspoon pepper	¼ cup grated *kefalotyri* cheese
½ teaspoon nutmeg	(or Parmesan)
¼ teaspoon cloves	

In heavy skillet melt butter; sauté onion a few minutes, then add
meat. Break up meat with fork; drain off fat; add salt, pepper, spices
and wine or beef stock. Cover and simmer 5 minutes. Stir in tomato
sauce; cover and simmer 45 minutes. Stir in cheese and mix well. Set
aside.

Macaroni:

½ pound large elbow macaroni	2 eggs, slightly beaten
3 quarts boiling water	½ cup grated *kefalotyri* cheese
1 tablespoon salt	(or Parmesan)
¼ cup butter	

Cook macaroni in boiling salted water until not quite tender. Drain;
rinse pan to wash away starch and melt butter in same pan. Return
drained macaroni and stir to mix in butter. Add eggs and cheese and
stir until mixed. Set aside.

Cream Sauce:

¼ cup butter	¼ teaspoon nutmeg
1 tablespoon flour	3 whole eggs plus 3 yolks
4 cups milk	¼ cup grated *kefalotyri* cheese
1 teaspoon salt	(or Parmesan)

Melt butter. Stir in flour. Remove from heat and add milk with salt and nutmeg. Stir and return to low heat, cooking until mixture thickens a little. Beat eggs and yolks well and add to cream sauce, beating until smooth. Add cheese and beat until smooth.

Using a buttered 8-x-8-x-2-inch pan, assemble layers as follows with ¾ cup grated *kefalotyri* cheese (or Parmesan): ½ macaroni, ¼ cup grated cheese, all the meat sauce, 4 tablespoons cream sauce, remaining macaroni, ¼ cup grated cheese, remaining cream sauce, and remaining cheese. Bake at 350 degrees for 40 minutes, or until knife inserted in center comes out clean. Let stand in warm place, until *pastichio* firms up. Return to oven to reheat before serving. If desired, freeze before baking. To bake, return to room temperature and follow directions.

ᛞ

F / R2

SOUTHWESTERN POT ROAST

6 servings

One 3-pound brisket of beef, or chuck roast	2 cloves garlic, minced
Salt and freshly ground black pepper to taste	1½ teaspoons paprika
	1 tablespoon canned, or fresh,
1 medium onion, sliced and separated into rings	green *chile* peppers, chopped (more if you like it hotter)
	1 tablespoon brown sugar

Trim off excess fat from meat. Brown it on both sides in its own fat. Season with salt and pepper. Add onion and garlic and sauté until limp. Add remaining ingredients. Cover and cook over very low heat so meat just barely simmers, turning occasionally. Cook until tender, about 3 hours.

Meat can be frozen or refrigerated. To serve, remove fat layer, return the roast to room temperature, slice and reheat slowly in its own liquid.

❧

R3

PICKLED TONGUE

6 servings

1 fresh beef tongue, about 3 pounds
1 tablespoon Mixed Pickling Spice (page 46)
1 clove garlic, peeled and halved

Cover tongue with water; add pickling spices and garlic. Cover and simmer gently for 2½ to 3 hours, until tongue is fork-tender. Drain. When it is cool enough to handle, skin and trim off gristle and small bones. Slice tongue portion; serve hot or cold.

❧

R1

PIQUANT TONGUE

3 servings

3 cups cooked Pickled Tongue (above), cut in slivers or pieces
2 anchovy fillets, rinsed and drained
1 tablespoon pine nuts
1 clove garlic, cut up

½ teaspoon capers
½ slice white bread, soaked in water and squeezed
6 tablespoons olive oil
2 tablespoons red wine vinegar
Freshly ground black pepper

Combine anchovies, pine nuts, garlic, capers and bread. Either pound to a paste in a mortar with a pestle, puree in blender or mash with wooden spoon in wooden bowl. Add the oil and vinegar alternately to make a smooth blended paste. Season with pepper. Combine with tongue and adjust seasonings. Serve cold.

ℛℓ

ZUCCHINI BOATS

4 servings

4 medium zucchini (about 2 pounds)	½ teaspoon Worcestershire sauce
½ pound spicy hot pork sausage	¼ cup fine cracker crumbs
¼ cup chopped onion	1 slightly beaten egg
1 clove garlic, minced	Salt and pepper to taste
½ cup freshly grated Parmesan cheese	¼ teaspoon dried thyme

Cook whole zucchini in boiling salted water until barely tender, 7 to 10 minutes. Cut in half lengthwise and scoop out pulp; mash the pulp, reserving the shell.

In a skillet cook the sausage. Drain off fat and add onion and garlic to the skillet, and cook until onion is soft. Stir in drained, mashed zucchini pulp. Reserve 2 tablespoons Parmesan cheese; mix all remaining ingredients together with zucchini mixture. Spoon into zucchini shells. Place in shallow baking dish. Refrigerate, if desired. To serve, sprinkle with reserved cheese and bake at 350 degrees for 25 to 30 minutes, or until heated through.

❦

LEG OF LAMB

6 servings

If you have been thinking about serving this dish enough in advance, you can insert slivers from 4 cloves of garlic into small incisions all over the leg a day or two before roasting.

6- or 7-pound whole leg of lamb
1 carrot, scraped and cut in
 large slices
1 onion, peeled and cut in large
 slices

1 cup Beef Stock or broth
 (page 89)
4 cloves garlic

Let lamb sit at room temperature for 30 minutes before roasting. Place in roasting pan with onion and carrot and roast at 325 degrees for 2 to 2½ hours, for medium-rare. For better-done meat, allow another 30 minutes or so. When lamb is cooked, allow to sit for 20 minutes so juices will be reabsorbed. While lamb is being carved, remove as much grease as possible from the juices in the pan. Discard onion and carrot and add the broth and reduce the liquid slightly by boiling. Pass gravy separately.

❦

F / R2

BARBECUED PORK

8 servings

2 pounds boneless pork
 tenderloin, or butt
1½ tablespoons soy sauce
2½ tablespoons hoisin sauce
1 tablespoon dry sherry

1 tablespoon honey
1 teaspoon sugar
Generous pinch of Five Spice
 Powder (page 39)
Additional honey

Combine all the ingredients but the pork. Cut the pork into strips about 1½ to 2 inches wide, 2 inches thick and 3 to 5 inches long.

Rub all sides of pork strips with marinade mixture and marinate overnight, turning pork strips in marinade occasionally. Using S-curved curtain hooks, hang the strips of pork from the hooks and hang the hooks from a rack in the oven set at the highest level. (The length of the pork strips will depend on the height of your oven!) Set a pan of water in the bottom of the oven, to catch the drippings from the pork. Roast at 425 degrees for 15 minutes. Reduce heat to 325 degrees and roast for 15 to 20 minutes longer, until pork is thoroughly cooked. Immediately upon removing from oven, brush with honey. Refrigerate or freeze, if desired. If frozen or refrigerated, reheat in foil before serving.

Serve warm or at room temperature, sliced thinly against the grain. Pass remaining marinade, hot mustard, soy sauce or plum sauce separately.

ಀ

MO SHU RO PORK

3 or 4 servings

Known as *moo shi* pork, this dish really cannot be made successfully without access to Chinese ingredients.

10 tiger-lily buds	2 tablespoons peanut oil
2 medium dried Chinese mushrooms	½ cup lean shredded pork
1 tablespoon tree ears	2 tablespoons dark Chinese soy sauce, or Japanese soy sauce
½ cup fresh bean sprouts	1 teaspoon sugar
1 scallion	6 to 8 Chinese pancakes
1 or 2 slices fresh ginger root	("doilies")
2 eggs	Hoisin sauce

In advance soak tiger-lily buds, mushrooms and tree ears in 1 cup warm water for 20 minutes. Wash and drain. Wash and drain bean sprouts. Shred mushrooms and scallion stalk, cutting green part into

2-inch sections. Mince ginger root. Beat the eggs and stir 1 tablespoon oil into egg mixture.

When ready to serve, heat remaining oil in wok or skillet over high heat. Add ginger and cook 30 seconds. Add shredded pork and stir about 2 minutes. Add 2 tablespoons soy sauce and 1 teaspoon sugar and stir a few more times. Add ginger, tiger-lily buds, mushrooms and tree ears and mix well. Add 2 tablespoons water and bring to boil. Set aside.

Add eggs to pan. Scramble quickly. Add bean sprouts and mix thoroughly. Combine with pork mixture and serve hot with doilies.

To heat doilies, steam them.

Put filling in doilies and roll up, like cigarettes. Serve with hoisin sauce.

ༀ

F / R2

GUISADO

This is a Mexican stew from **La Cocina in Aspen, Colorado,** with a few home touches.

2 pounds diced very lean pork
Salt and freshly ground black
    pepper to taste
1 large onion, diced
2 small cloves garlic, minced
2 (28-ounce) cans tomatoes
3 tablespoons chopped green
    chiles (more if you like the
    stew hotter)
¼ cup minced parsley

2 teaspoons cumin
2 teaspoons dried oregano
1 teaspoon dried thyme
1 small hot dried red pepper,
    minced, seeds removed
2 cups Chicken Stock or
    bouillon (page 90)
5 potatoes, peeled, diced and
    cooked

Brown the meat in its own fat. Season with salt and pepper. Sauté onion and garlic in the same pan until golden. Add all of remaining ingredients but the potatoes. Cover and simmer for 2 hours. Adjust seasonings during cooking. Add potatoes during last 20 minutes of cooking. If desired, prepare ahead but do not add potatoes if freezing. To serve, if frozen, defrost, adjust seasonings; add potatoes and cook 20 minutes.

ઌ

R1

CHINESE BARBECUED RIBS

6 servings

¾ cup hoisin sauce
3 tablespoons yellow bean paste
1½ tablespoons black Chinese soy sauce, or Japanese soy sauce

1½ tablespoons brown sugar
1 tablespoon fresh ginger, minced
6 pounds lean spareribs

Combine all ingredients but spareribs. Place spareribs in water to cover and bring to boil; boil for 30 minutes. Drain and dry ribs. Spread ⅔ of the hoisin-paste mixture over ribs, on both sides. Allow to marinate in this paste for at least 2 hours, or overnight if desired, in the refrigerator. To serve, grill ribs 8 to 10 inches from hot coals, about 20 minutes, brushing frequently with remaining hoisin mixture. Ribs are ready when the juice between 2 ribs that have been cut runs clear. Cut ribs into serving pieces and serve with hot mustard, if desired.

❧ VII ❦

MEATLESS MAIN DISHES

❧

R1

BROCCOLI RICE CASSEROLE

10 servings

This dish was served at the Food Day celebration in 1977 at the White House. The entire meal was vegetarian, which made the beef industry so angry it fired off a telegram to President Carter, demanding that meat be included. The casserole is excellent as a combination side dish or as a main dish for a vegetarian meal. This is an adapted version.

1½ cups brown rice
Dash of salt
  2 tablespoons oil
  1 large onion, chopped
  2 large cloves garlic, minced
  ½ teaspoon dillweed
  1 teaspoon thyme
  1 teaspoon oregano
  ½ bunch parsley, chopped
  ½ pound mushrooms, sliced

1 green pepper, sliced
2 pounds broccoli,
   approximately; tough stalks
   removed, remainder sliced
   thin
½ cup unsalted cashews
½ pound Gruyère cheese, grated
¼ cup grated Parmesan cheese
½ pint sour cream

In heavy saucepan with tight-fitting lid combine rice with 3 cups water and dash of salt. Bring to boil; reduce heat and simmer for about 45 minutes, until all water is absorbed. Do not stir rice while it cooks.

Heat oil in large frying pan. Sauté onion, garlic, dill, thyme and oregano until onion starts to wilt. Then add parsley, mushrooms and green pepper. Stir 1 or 2 minutes and add broccoli. Stir often. As soon as broccoli changes color and becomes tender, but is still crisp, add nuts and remove from heat.

Spread cooked rice in 9-x-13-inch baking dish. Cover with vegetable-nut mixture, then with cheeses, and finally with sour cream. Bake for 20 minutes at 350 degrees, until mixture is bubbly and cheese has melted.

Dish can be assembled in advance and refrigerated. To serve, return to room temperature and bake about 25 or 30 minutes.

ℰ

F / R2

BULGUR CASSEROLE

10 or 12 servings

4 tablespoons oil	1 (1-pound, 12-ounce) can
2 cups chopped onion	tomatoes
3 cloves garlic, finely chopped	1 cup dry sherry
¼ pound fresh mushrooms,	2 teaspoons oregano
chopped	Salt and pepper to taste
1½ cups bulgur (cracked wheat)	2 cups grated Cheddar cheese
2 cups sliced black olives	4 tablespoons chopped parsley
	Paprika

Heat oil in skillet. Sauté onion, garlic and mushrooms in hot oil until onion is golden. Add bulgur, olives, tomatoes, sherry, oregano, salt and pepper. Mix well; bring to boil and pour into 4-quart casserole. Refrigerate or freeze, if desired. When ready to serve, return to room temperature, cover and bake at 375 degrees for 20 to 30 minutes, until mixture is heated through. Uncover, sprinkle with cheese and continue baking for 15 minutes, until cheese melts. Sprinkle with parsley and paprika and serve.

NOTE: This dish can be made nonvegetarian by browning 2 pounds of ground beef in its own fat, then adding onion, mushrooms and garlic and sautéing until onions are golden.

✌

R1

CHILAQUILES

8 servings

¼ pound plus 4 tablespoons
  butter
1 medium onion, chopped
1 medium tomato, chopped
4 cups finely chopped fresh,
  frozen or dried green
  medium-hot *chiles* *

13-ounce can evaporated milk
24 ounces sour cream
Salt to taste
 2 dozen corn tortillas

Heat 4 tablespoons butter in large skillet. Add onion, tomato and *chiles*. Sauté about 10 minutes, until onion is softened. Add milk and bring to a boil. Reduce heat and stir in sour cream; do not allow to boil.

Meanwhile heat remaining butter, a few tablespoons at a time, in a large skillet. Add a few tortillas in a single layer, and allow to warm and soften on both sides. Stack tortillas until ready to use. In dish deep enough to hold tortillas stacked with *chile* sauce between them, place one tortilla, top with about 1 tablespoon *chile* mixture, and spread to cover tortilla. Top with another tortilla and then more *chile*, using up all tortillas and *chile*, ending with *chile* mixture. If served immediately, cover with foil and heat about 15 minutes at 350 degrees.

To serve the next day, refrigerate. To heat, place dish in pan of water about 1 inch deep. Bake at 250 degrees, covered, about 1 hour, until heated through.

---

* *Chiles* used in New Mexico, from where this recipe comes, are difficult to find here. They are 5 to 8 inches long, range from medium to hot in flavor and are sometimes called California *chiles*. To substitute, combine about 3 cups chopped bell peppers and one cup chopped hot *chiles*, such as jalapeños.

ℰ

R1

ENCHILADAS

2 dozen

3 tablespoons oil
1 cup mild pure red *chile*
    powder *
2 tablespoons flour
4 cups water
Salt to taste
Pinch of sugar

2 dozen corn tortillas
½ cup oil
1½ cups grated Muenster or
    Monterey Jack cheese
½ cup finely chopped onion
13-ounce can evaporated milk,
    or 1½ cups sour cream

Heat 3 tablespoons oil in skillet. Combine *chile* powder and flour and stir into oil until well mixed. Remove from heat and gradually add water until mixture is smooth. Return to heat; add salt and sugar and simmer for 10 minutes.

In separate skillet heat ½ cup oil, a few tablespoons at a time. Dip tortillas into oil on both sides, just long enough to warm and soften. Drain on absorbent paper and then dip each tortilla in chili mixture and shake to drain. In center of each tortilla place 1 tablespoon cheese and 1 teaspoon onion. Roll tortillas into tube and place close together, seam side down, in shallow oblong baking dish. Combine remaining chili mixture with evaporated milk and pour over enchiladas (rolled tortillas). If served immediately, cover with foil and bake at 350 degrees for 20 to 30 minutes.

To serve the next day, refrigerate. Then bake at 250 degrees about 1 hour, or until heated through.

---

* Pure *chile* powder is available in Spanish markets. It is not the same as the chili powder found in supermarkets, which is a mixture of spices.

FRENCH MUSHROOM TARTE

6 servings

F / R2

Tarte Pastry:

2 cups flour, sifted

1 teaspoon salt

1½ sticks sweet butter, softened

⅓ cup ice water

Into large bowl sift flour and salt. Cut in the butter and work mixture with your fingers until it resembles cornmeal. Add the water and work to firm dough quickly. Knead slightly on floured surface. Turn out on lightly floured board and roll into ¼-inch-thick circle. Line either a 10-inch pie plate or flan ring on a cookie sheet with the pastry, making a fluted edge and cutting off the excess. Prick bottom and sides with fork. Line with a piece of buttered wax paper and weight with dry rice or beans to prevent bottom crust from puffing up. Bake at 375 degrees for 30 minutes. Remove flan ring, if used, paper and rice and bake 10 minutes more, until golden brown.

The tarte may be prepared a couple of days ahead, wrapped well after cooling, and held at room temperature until serving time; or it may be made several weeks ahead and frozen. Defrost before filling.

R1

Tarte Filling:

3 tablespoons butter

3 tablespoons flour

¾ cup milk

½ cup heavy cream

2 egg yolks, lightly beaten

1 pound fresh mushrooms, cut in large dice

2 tablespoons shallots, finely minced

2 tablespoons butter

1 teaspoon lemon juice

1 teaspoon salt

Freshly ground pepper

2 cups grated Gruyère cheese

Melt the butter in saucepan; stir in flour until blended and cook over low heat for a minute or two. Remove from heat and stir in milk, blending well. Cook until mixture thickens. Stir in cream and egg yolks.

Meanwhile, sauté mushrooms and shallots in 2 tablespoons butter, cooking over high heat until liquid has evaporated. Stir in lemon juice. Add to cream sauce with salt, pepper and 1 cup cheese. Pour into tarte shell; sprinkle with remaining cheese and bake at 350 degrees for 15 to 20 minutes, until mixture bubbles and cheese begins to brown. Serve hot.

Filling may be prepared a day ahead, refrigerated and then carefully reheated before being poured into tarte shell for baking.

F / Rl

ITALIAN-AMERICAN EGGPLANT

6 servings

4 tablespoons olive oil	⅔ cup water
1 large onion, finely chopped	¾ cup dry red wine
1 large clove garlic, minced	1 teaspoon basil
Salt and freshly ground pepper to taste	1 teaspoon oregano
	1 teaspoon Worcestershire sauce
1 medium eggplant, peeled and sliced	8 ounces mozzarella cheese, sliced
1 (6-ounce) can tomato paste	½ cup grated Parmesan cheese

In 2 tablespoons of oil, sauté the onion and garlic until onion is limp. Season with salt and pepper. Meanwhile, sauté eggplant slices in remaining oil on both sides, until limp and golden. Line a shallow casserole with eggplant slices.

Add the tomato paste, water, wine, basil, oregano and Worcestershire to onion mixture and stir, heating through. Spoon the mixture over the eggplant slices. Top with slices of mozzarella and sprinkle with Parmesan. Bake at 325 degrees for 20 minutes, until cheese is melted and bubbly.

Can be made ahead and refrigerated or frozen. To serve, return to room temperature and bake at 325 degrees for 30 to 40 minutes.

Ꮹ

R1

KOLOKITHOPITA

Approximately 24 pieces

This is a Greek squash pie.

3 pounds zucchini or yellow squash, grated	¾ pound feta cheese, crumbled
½ teaspoon salt	1 tablespoon chopped parsley
8 eggs, lightly beaten	¼ pound butter, melted
¼ cup farina	½ pound *phyllo*
Dash of pepper	½ pound butter, melted

Scrub, dry and grate squash. Add salt. Let stand for 15 minutes, then squeeze to remove as much liquid as possible. Add eggs, farina, pepper, cheese, parsley, ¼ pound melted butter. Mix well.

Use oblong pan approximately 9-x-13 inches and at least 2 inches deep. With soft pastry brush, butter bottom and sides. Lay 1 *phyllo* at a time, buttering each well, and use 6 for the bottom. Spread the squash mixture and add 8 more *phyllo*, buttering each one as well as top one. Bake at 350 degrees for 15 minutes, lower to 325 degrees and bake for another 30 minutes, or until top is golden brown.

Allow to cool for about 5 minutes; cut into 2-inch squares and serve. If served much later or refrigerated, reheat in oven to restore crispness to pastry.

❧

R2

POLENTA WITH TOMATO SAUCE

6 servings

1½ cups salted water
1½ cups vegetable stock
1½ cups polenta, or finely
    ground yellow cornmeal
6 tablespoons butter
½ cup freshly grated Parmesan
    or Romano cheese
½ pound fresh mushrooms,
    sliced

2 tablespoons flour
2 cups milk
Salt and pepper to taste
Pinch of nutmeg
1 cup diced canned tomatoes,
    drained
Additional Parmesan for
    topping

Bring water and stock to boil; slowly add polenta, stirring constantly with a wooden spoon until all the lumps disappear. Continue cooking over low heat for about 10 minutes, until all the moisture has evaporated and the polenta comes away from the sides of the pan. Add 2 tablespoons butter and ¼ cup cheese. Mix and spread in a 9-x-11-inch shallow buttered baking pan, so mixture is approximately ½ inch thick; cool. Sauté mushrooms in 2 tablespoons butter. In another pan, melt remaining butter; stir in flour. Stir in milk gradually with salt, pepper and nutmeg. Cook, stirring, until sauce is thickened. Add remaining cheese, mushrooms and tomatoes.

Turn polenta out of pan and slice sideways into 2 layers. Put 1 layer into a buttered pan a little larger than the polenta itself. Cover with half the sauce. Add the second layer and top with remaining sauce. Sprinkle with additional Parmesan cheese and refrigerate, if desired.

To serve, return to room temperature and bake at 375 degrees for about 20 to 25 minutes, until sauce is bubbly and cheese is browned.

❧

R1

RIGATONI WITH BROCCOLI

8 to 10 servings as pasta course, or 12 as side dish

½ pound fresh mushrooms,
  sliced
2 tablespoons butter
1½ cups light cream
1 cup cooked broccoli, finely
  chopped
1 cup canned Italian plum
  tomatoes, chopped

½ teaspoon oregano
½ teaspoon basil
1 pound rigatoni
Freshly ground black pepper
Salt to taste
¼ cup freshly grated Parmesan
  cheese

Sauté mushrooms in butter for 5 minutes. Combine them with cream, broccoli, tomatoes, oregano and basil. Cook for about 5 minutes. Refrigerate if prepared ahead.

Cook rigatoni in boiling salted water for about 18 minutes, or until just tender; drain. Place rigatoni in hot sauce. Season to taste with salt and pepper. Remove from heat and add cheese. Mix well and serve.

❧

SCRAMBLED EGG FOO YONG

6 servings

This is the kind of dish into which you can put any appropriate vegetable scraps. If you want to turn it into a meat dish, add shrimp, chicken, turkey.

10 tablespoons butter
1 large onion, chopped
3 stalks celery, chopped
¼ pound mushrooms, chopped

Salt and freshly ground black
  pepper
1 cup bean sprouts
12 eggs, beaten

Heat 6 tablespoons butter in large skillet. Sauté onion and celery in butter until almost tender. Add mushrooms and sauté a minute or two longer. Add bean sprouts. Stir cooked vegetables into beaten eggs. Add salt and pepper to taste. Heat 4 tablespoons butter in same skillet. Cook and stir egg mixture in skillet until cooked, but still moist.

RI

SEASHELLS AND EGGPLANT

4 servings as main dish; 12 as side dish

1 large eggplant, skin on, finely diced
1 cup minced celery
4 tablespoons olive oil
1 onion, finely chopped
1 tablespoon minced parsley
1 clove garlic, minced
1 teaspoon oregano
1 teaspoon thyme
2 tablespoons unsalted butter
2 cups canned Italian plum tomatoes, finely diced
Salt and freshly ground black pepper to taste
1 pound small macaroni shells
Freshly grated Parmesan or Romano cheese

Soak eggplant in salt water for 1 hour. Drain thoroughly in colander.

Sauté celery in 2 tablespoons oil for about 5 minutes; add onion, parsley, garlic, oregano and thyme. Cook 5 minutes more.

In another pan sauté the eggplant in remaining oil plus butter until soft. Combine all vegetables. Add the tomatoes with their juice and bring to rapid boil.

At this point the dish may be refrigerated, if desired. To serve, simmer the vegetables over low heat for about one hour. Season with salt and pepper.

Cook shells in boiling salted water as directed on package, just until tender. Drain and add to hot sauce; heat through. Serve topped with generous amounts of freshly grated cheese.

❦

R1

SPINACH TARTE

30 squares for hors d'oeuvres, or 6 to 8 as side dish

This can be served hot as a side dish, or it can be served cold or slightly warm as an hors d'oeuvre.

1 pound fresh spinach, or 1 (10-ounce) package frozen spinach, defrosted
2 tablespoons butter
1½ cups chopped onion
½ pint yogurt and ½ pint sour
. cream
4 ounces grated sharp Cheddar cheese

4 ounces (¼ pound) fresh mushrooms, sliced
3 eggs, lightly beaten
1 teaspoon Worcestershire sauce
⅛ teaspoon nutmeg
Salt to taste

If using fresh spinach, cook quickly in covered pot without liquid until it has wilted. Drain thoroughly to remove excess moisture. If using frozen spinach, defrost and squeeze out liquid.

In butter, sauté onions until golden. Combine all of ingredients in 9-x-12-inch baking dish.

Refrigerate if desired. To serve, return to room temperature and bake at 350 degrees for about 40 minutes, until eggs are set and mixture is firm.

Serve hot or cold.

❧

R1

TABBOULEH

6 to 8 servings

1 cup bulgur (cracked wheat)
3 medium tomatoes, chopped
1 bunch green onions, chopped
3 cups chopped parsley
¼ cup fresh mint, chopped
½ cup olive oil

4 to 6 tablespoons lemon juice
Salt and freshly ground black
   pepper to taste
Lettuce leaves
Cinnamon

Wash the bulgur; cover with hot water and allow to stand for 30 minutes. Drain thoroughly and then squeeze dry with hands. Chop the vegetables and mint together. Beat in the oil, lemon juice, salt and pepper, and mix with bulgur until well blended. Serve in lettuce-lined salad bowl, preferably glass, sprinkled with cinnamon. Or pass cinnamon separately.

❧

R1

TORTILLA DE SPINACA (SPINACH CASSEROLE)

12 servings as main dish

Sara Clapp made this dish for a story I was doing about her and her cooking, which is a mixture of her heritage—Greek, Sephardic Jewish, and Argentine. Note what it says for garlic: not a clove, but a whole head. You are not overwhelmed by it.

6 (10-ounce) packages fresh or frozen spinach
10 slices whole-wheat bread
1 head garlic, peeled and finely chopped
2 bunches spring onions, thinly sliced
1 pound mushrooms, chopped
3 tablespoons oil
Salt and freshly ground black pepper to taste
1 tablespoon dried dillweed, or 3 tablespoons chopped fresh dill

2½ teaspoons dried oregano
1 teaspoon nutmeg
1 teaspoon paprika
1 tablespoon dried mint leaves, or 3 tablespoons chopped fresh mint
6 eggs, slightly beaten
½ cup grated Parmesan cheese
Milk, if needed
4 tablespoons melted butter
1 cup bread crumbs

If spinach is frozen, defrost and squeeze out liquid into a measuring cup. Cook fresh spinach without adding additional water, just until it wilts. Drain, reserving liquid. Moisten bread with water; then squeeze out water. Sauté garlic, onions and mushrooms in 2 tablespoons oil until onions soften. Add the salt, pepper, dill, oregano, nutmeg, paprika and mint and mix well. Remove from pan. Heat remaining tablespoon oil and sauté spinach in it briefly. Combine spinach, bread, garlic mixture, eggs and cheese. Add enough milk to spinach juices, if necessary, to make 2 cups. Mix with spinach. Grease a 3- to 3½-quart shallow baking dish and spoon in spinach mixture. Melt 4 tablespoons butter; add bread crumbs and stir to moisten thoroughly. Sprinkle buttered crumbs over top of spinach.

Refrigerate if desired. To serve, return to room temperature and bake at 350 degrees for 45 to 60 minutes, until mixture is bubbly and hot. Cut into squares and serve.

NOTE: This dish also may be served on the side to 20 people. It can be served cold as an appetizer with feta cheese, tomatoes and onion slices, Greek olives and Greek bread.

❧

RAREBIT FONDUE

Makes 2 cups

4 cups diced mild Cheddar
   cheese
2 teaspoons Worcestershire sauce
2 cloves garlic, minced

1 cup tomato puree
4 tablespoons dry sherry
Cubes of French bread

In heavy saucepan combine cheese, Worcestershire, garlic and tomato puree. Cook over low heat until cheese is melted and smooth. Stir in sherry and cook until well heated. Pour into fondue pot and keep warm. Spear bread on forks and dip in fondue or serve over toast.

❧

F / R1

RICOTTA RICE

6 servings

3 cups cooked brown rice
¼ cup finely chopped green
   onion
1½ cups ricotta cheese (creamed
   cottage cheese if ricotta is
   not available)

1 clove garlic, minced
½ pint sour cream
2 tablespoons milk
Few drops hot pepper sauce
Salt to taste
⅓ cup grated Parmesan cheese

Combine rice and onions. Blend ricotta, garlic, sour cream, milk, hot pepper sauce and salt. Stir into rice mixture. Turn into buttered 1½-quart casserole. Refrigerate or freeze, if desired. To serve, return to room temperature and sprinkle with Parmesan. Bake at 350 degrees for 25 minutes.

❧

F

INDIVIDUAL CHEESE SOUFFLÉS

4 servings

Soufflés which can be made ahead and frozen, popped directly from freezer to oven, then served. No last minute work!

2 tablespoons butter	1 cup hot milk
4 tablespoons flour	1½ cups grated sharp cheese:
½ teaspoon salt	Cheddar or Parmesan
¼ teaspoon pepper	6 eggs, separated
¼ teaspoon dry mustard	

Have ready four 1-pint (2-cup) soufflé dishes or six ½-pint (1-cup) soufflé dishes, or a combination of those. Line the dishes with aluminum foil, fitting as snugly as possible and allowing for a 5- or 6-inch overhang, which will be used to cover the soufflé tops during freezing and then act as collars during baking.

Melt butter. Blend in flour and seasonings and cook 1 minute. Remove from heat; slowly stir in hot milk until mixture is smooth. Cook and stir over medium heat until sauce thickens. Reduce heat, add cheese and stir until cheese is melted and blended. Cool for 5 minutes. Beat yolks well. Slowly add a little of the cooled cheese mixture to yolks, stirring vigorously. Then pour the remaining egg-yolk mixture into cheese mixture and mix well.

Beat egg whites until stiff but not dry. Fold whites into cheese base. Pour into soufflé dishes and freeze (up to 4 weeks). After mixture is frozen, remove soufflé dishes and wrap soufflés in foil.

To serve, return soufflés to soufflé dishes and make a collar out of foil. Bake at 300 degrees for 50 to 60 minutes.

ও

LOW-CAL LAST-MINUTE SOUFFLÉ

2 servings

4 eggs, separated
1½ cups coarsely grated sharp
   Cheddar cheese

2 tablespoons dry skim-milk
   powder
Salt and pepper to taste

Combine cheese and skim-milk powder with slightly beaten egg yolks. Season with salt and pepper. Beat whites stiffly with a pinch of salt. Fold into cheese mixture. Turn into ungreased 2-cup soufflé dish and bake at 425 degrees for 10 to 15 minutes, until soufflé is puffed and brown.

ও

F / R3

PASTA WITH THREE CHEESES

6 servings

2 to 3 tablespoons fine dry
   bread crumbs
12 ounces bow-tie noodles,
   cooked with salt and drained
2 tablespoons butter

4 ounces freshly grated
   Parmesan cheese
4 ounces Gruyère cheese, diced
5 ounces diced mozzarella
   cheese

Butter a shallow 3-quart baking dish; coat with bread crumbs.

Toss noodles with butter. Add cheeses and toss lightly, reserving a little Parmesan for top.

Turn half the noodle mixture into baking dish. Top with half of white sauce (see page 155). Repeat layers. Sprinkle remaining Parmesan on top. Bake at 350 degrees for about 25 minutes, or until hot and bubbly.

If desired, freeze before baking. To serve, return to room temperature and bake as directed.

White Sauce:

3 tablespoons butter
3 tablespoons flour
3 cups milk

Salt and pepper to taste
$\frac{1}{8}$ teaspoon nutmeg

Melt butter; remove from heat and stir in flour. Gradually add milk and return to heat. Cook, stirring, until mixture thickens. Season with salt, pepper and nutmeg.

❦ VIII ❦

VEGETABLES

৺

ASPARAGUS WITH BREAD-CRUMB SAUCE

8 servings

½ cup butter
4 tablespoons bread crumbs

4 pounds asparagus, cooked and
   drained

Melt butter; add crumbs. Cook and stir until crumbs are browned. Serve over hot asparagus.

৺

BAKED CHEESE GRITS

8 to 10 servings

1 cup grits
½ cup butter
3 cups grated sharp Cheddar
   cheese

4 eggs, separated
¼ cup light cream
Dash Worcestershire sauce
Salt and pepper to taste

Cook grits until thick and smooth according to package directions. Stir in butter, 2 cups cheese, slightly beaten yolks, cream, Worcestershire and seasoning. This can be done up to an hour ahead, but don't let mixture get cold.

When ready to bake beat whites until stiff; fold into grits. Spoon into greased 2-quart casserole. Bake at 350 degrees for 30 minutes; sprinkle top with remaining cheese and bake 15 minutes longer.

℞

F / Rl

BEA'S RATATOUILLE

12 servings

4 large eggplant (5 pounds), cut
  in 1-inch cubes
6 medium (5 pounds) zucchini,
  cut into 1/4-inch-thick slices
6 onions (2½ pounds), sliced
6 green peppers, cut in 1-inch
  pieces
5 cloves garlic, put through
  garlic press
15 sprigs fresh dill, or 2½ teaspoons dried dillweed

12 sprigs fresh parsley
2 teaspoons dried oregano
1 (2-pound, 3-ounce) can
  peeled Italian tomatoes
1½ tablespoons drained capers,
  optional
3 tablespoons salt
½ teaspoon freshly ground
  black pepper
¼ cup olive oil

Do not peel eggplant or zucchini. Remove tough stems from fresh dill. Place all ingredients in 1 or 2 large pots. Mix contents of pot(s) until they are coated well with oil and the seasonings are evenly distributed. Cover and bake at 350 degrees, stirring frequently in the beginning until vegetables soften and juices begin to flow. After that, stir occasionally and bake 2 hours. Leave cover off during last half-hour of cooking.

Or cook, covered, on top of stove about 1 hour, just below a simmer. Test for doneness. If soft, uncover, raise heat a little and simmer a half-hour to reduce liquid.

Serve hot or cold.

℞

BRAISED ENDIVE

8 servings

8 large endives, washed and
  drained
1 medium onion, sliced
⅓ cup butter

¾ cup Beef Stock (page 89),
  Chicken Stock (page 90) or
  vegetable stock
Salt and pepper to taste

Place the endives in a saucepan with the onion. Dot with the butter and cover with the stock. Season with salt and pepper. Cover and simmer over low heat about 30 minutes, until endives are tender and liquid is absorbed.

❧

BROCCOLI WITH WHITE WINE

4 servings

2 pounds fresh broccoli, tops only
1 large clove garlic, minced
3 tablespoons olive oil

1/4 teaspoon freshly ground black pepper
1/2 teaspoon salt
1 cup dry white wine

Ahead of time cut broccoli at point where all branches meet stems. (Use stems for soup.) Break up broccoli heads into individual branches. Cook garlic in hot oil for about 30 seconds. Toss broccoli in oil until well coated. Add pepper, salt and wine. Cover and simmer about 10 minutes, until tender. Serve with liquid from pan poured over.

❧

BRUSSELS SPROUTS WITH GREEN GRAPES

6 servings

1 quart Brussels sprouts
1 cup green grapes, seeded and halved
3 or 4 tablespoons butter

Salt and freshly ground black pepper to taste
1/2 cup heavy cream

Clean, strip off any yellow leaves and slice off ends of sprouts. Partially cook in boiling water until not quite tender, about 5 minutes. Drain. Return well-drained sprouts, grapes and 2 tablespoons butter to pan. Season with salt and pepper and heat until butter is melted and sizzling. Pour in cream; reduce heat to low and cook sprouts until cream has almost evaporated completely, about 10 minutes. Dot with 1 or 2 tablespoons more butter. Adjust seasonings and serve.

F / R2

CIDER RICE PILAF

4 servings

6 tablespoons butter	⅓ cup chopped onion
1 cup brown rice	½ cup chopped celery
Salt and freshly ground black pepper to taste	¼ cup chopped parsley
	⅛ teaspoon dried rosemary
1 teaspoon grated orange peel	2½ to 3 cups apple cider

In skillet melt the butter. Add rice and cook slowly, stirring, until rice is golden. Add salt, pepper, orange peel, onion and celery; continue sautéing for about 5 minutes. Add 3 tablespoons parsley and the rosemary.

In saucepan bring cider to boil; stir into rice. Cook rice, tightly covered, over low heat about 1 hour, or until all of liquid is absorbed and rice is tender. Serve topped with remaining parsley.

You can also refrigerate or freeze before cooking, if desired. When ready to serve, return to room temperature. Some of the liquid will be absorbed and the rice partially cooked. Continue cooking until rice is tender. Top with parsley and serve.

CORN ROAST IN FOIL

10 ears

By this method it is possible to make old corn taste pretty good.

1 quart water	¼ pound, or more, melted butter
2 tablespoons sugar	
10 ears corn	Seasoned Salt (page 38) or table salt

Combine water and sugar and soak corn in mixture for 15 minutes. Remove and wrap each ear, still in husks, in piece of aluminum foil.

Place foil-wrapped corn on grill and cook for 15 minutes, turning often. Remove foil, strip corn of husks (unless your hands are very tough, you will need to wear gloves) and roll corn in shallow platter of melted butter. Season with salt, if desired.

❧

F / R1

CRACKED WHEAT (BULGUR) WITH PEACHES

6 to 8 servings

This is excellent with poultry and is enough to stuff a 10-pound goose or 2 (5-pound) chickens.

½ pound dried peaches, cut in quarters, or half dried apples and half peaches	2 celery stalks, chopped
	2 medium onions, chopped
	⅓ cup pine nuts
½ cup tawny port or apple cider	1 teaspoon dried sage
1 cup cracked wheat (bulgur)	Salt and freshly ground black pepper
2 cups cold water	
¼ cup butter	

Soak the cut-up peaches in the wine overnight. Drain and reserve any wine not absorbed. Soak the cracked wheat in the cold water for 2 hours (overnight if desired) until all the liquid is absorbed.

Melt the butter; sauté the celery and onions until tender and lightly golden. Remove from heat; add the cracked wheat, peaches, pine nuts, sage, salt and pepper. Place in a large casserole and bake at 350 degrees for 45 minutes, until heated through. Stir once or twice.

If desired, prepare ahead, refrigerate or freeze until serving time. Return to room temperature and bake as directed.

NOTE: If you are serving this dish with poultry, use the reserved port with stock to baste bird(s).

❧

DRY SAUTÉED STRING BEANS

4 servings

A wonderful Szechuan vegetable dish

2 pounds fresh beans, trimmed
Peanut or soy oil for deep frying
2 tablespoons soy oil
2 to 3 tablespoons ground pork
2 teaspoons Szechuan pickle
  (Szechuan preserved
  vegetables, finely chopped)
2 tablespoons chicken broth or
  water
2 tablespoons dry sherry

½ teaspoon ground ginger
½ teaspoon minced garlic
2 tablespoons hoisin sauce
1 tablespoon dark soy sauce
¼ teaspoon white pepper
2½ teaspoons oyster sauce
1 to 1½ teaspoons red *chile*
  paste or sauce
1 tablespoon spring onions
1 teaspoon sesame oil

Deep-fry green beans at 325 degrees for one minute in peanut or soy oil. When skins of beans get wrinkled, but before they burst, the beans are ready; drain thoroughly.

Heat 2 tablespoons soy oil in wok or heavy skillet until very hot. Add pork and pickle and stir to coat meat with oil. Add chicken broth and cook until pork browns. Then add sherry, ginger, garlic, hoisin sauce, soy, pepper, oyster sauce and *chile* paste. Stir well. Add green beans and stir. Add spring onions and sesame oil just before serving.

❧

FIDEO (VERMICELLI)

3 to 4 servings

This is a New Mexican version of a Mexican dish and will go well with any Mexican food, but is also a good accompaniment to chicken, beef or fish.

8-ounce package vermicelli (thin spaghetti)

2 tablespoons oil

2 small onions, chopped fine

2 small tomatoes, chopped fine

2 cloves garlic, minced

1½ cups Chicken Stock or broth (page 90)

Brown vermicelli in hot oil very slowly. Drain vermicelli on absorbent paper and place in pot with cover. Sauté onion, tomato and garlic in oil remaining in pan until onion is tender. Combine with broth and salt to taste. Pour over vermicelli. Cover and cook slowly on top of stove until all the liquid is absorbed and vermicelli is tender.

ᵉ

F / R2

FRUITED BULGUR

10 servings

Very good with poultry

¼ cup butter

1 large onion, minced

¾ cup slivered blanched almonds

1 pound cracked wheat (bulgur)

4½ cups Beef Stock (page 89) or Chicken Stock (page 90)

¾ cup dried apricots, cut up

4 tablespoons currants

Melt the butter in a skillet. Sauté the onion and almonds in the butter until golden. Add the bulgur and cook until bulgur begins to turn golden. Add the stock, apricots and currants and place in casserole. Bake at 350 degrees for 40 to 45 minutes, until all liquid is absorbed. Serve.

You can also prepare ahead up to baking, then refrigerate or freeze. To serve, return to room temperature and bake at 350 degrees about 30 minutes, until heated through.

❧

ʀl

GALUSKA

6 servings

A variation on Hungarian noodles from Paulette Fono and the restaurant, Paprikas Fono, in San Francisco she owns with her husband.

3 cups flour	3 quarts of water
2 tablespoons salt	4 tablespoons butter, melted
3 whole eggs	1 cup shredded sharp cheese,
1 cup water	optional
1 teaspoon oil	

Place flour and 1 tablespoon of salt into large mixing bowl and mix well with wooden spoon. Add eggs and water, using wooden spoon and a beating motion. Mix until evenly blended and no large lumps of egg and flour remain. Allow 2 minutes for mixing. Scrape off sides of bowl and pour a teaspoon of oil on top of dough to prevent from drying.

In large pot, bring 3 quarts of water and 1 tablespoon of salt to boil. Take small cutting board. Place ⅓ of dough on it. Dip knife into boiling water and cut a narrow strip of dough approximately ¼ inch wide. Lean cutting board over top of pot and cut dough quickly into 1- or 2-inch pieces, with cutting and scraping motion, scraping dough off board, directly into boiling water. Dip knife frequently into boiling water. Repeat until all dough is gone.

Wait until *galuska* come to top of water. Allow to boil briefly. Stir with slotted spoon, then take *galuska* out with this spoon and quickly wash with cold water; drain. Place in ovenproof serving dish. Dribble some melted butter on top of *galuska*. Repeat until all dough is used up. Sprinkle with cheese, if desired. Mix *galuska* thoroughly so that it is well coated with butter and cheese. Serve immediately, or refrigerate. Reheat in same dish by placing *galuska* (covered) in a 350-degree oven for 25 to 30 minutes.

ళ

GRILLED POTATO PACKAGES

4 to 6 servings

4 medium potatoes, pared and
 cut in ½-inch cubes
1 cup chopped onion
½ cup coarsely chopped green
 pepper

Salt and pepper to taste
¼ teaspoon caraway seed
¼ cup butter

Place potatoes in center of 18-x-22-inch rectangle of heavy-duty aluminum foil. Add onion and green pepper. Season with salt, pepper and caraway. Dot with butter. Seal securely. Place foil package, seam side down, on grill 5 inches from coals. Grill 20 minutes. Turn package and grill 20 minutes longer, or until potatoes are done. Toss lightly with fork and serve. (Indoors, bake in foil at 425 degrees for about 40 minutes.)

ళ

Rl

HOT HERBED TOMATOES

6 servings

1½ pints cherry tomatoes
 6 tablespoons finely minced
 onion
 1 large clove garlic, finely
 minced
 6 tablespoons chopped parsley

⅓ teaspoon dried thyme
¾ cup soft bread crumbs
¾ teaspoon salt
Dash pepper
 6 tablespoons olive oil or salad
 oil

Stem tomatoes and wash; drain. Combine remaining ingredients; mix well. Arrange tomatoes in single layer in lightly oiled, shallow baking dish. Sprinkle bread-crumb mixture over tomatoes. Refrigerate, if desired. To serve, return to room temperature and bake at 425 degrees for 6 to 8 minutes, or until tomatoes are softened.

~

F / R2

MUENSTER-STUFFED POTATOES

12 servings

6 baking potatoes
1 cup firmly packed, coarsely grated Muenster cheese
1 clove garlic, crushed
10 tablespoons melted butter

1 cup milk
Salt and freshly ground black pepper to taste
1/3 cup fine bread crumbs

Scrub potatoes and bake at 400 degrees for about 45 to 50 minutes, or until done. Cut potatoes in half lengthwise and scoop out potato. Reserve shells.

In a bowl, mash potatoes or press through ricer. While hot, add the cheese, garlic and 8 tablespoons (1/2 cup) butter. Gradually stir in milk until potatoes are light and fluffy. Season with salt and pepper. Spoon into potato shells. Combine bread crumbs with 2 tablespoons butter and pepper. Spoon mixture over potatoes, and refrigerate or freeze, if desired.

To serve, return to room temperature and bake at 350 degrees for 25 to 30 minutes.

~

PARSLEY NOODLES

6 servings

1 pound broad egg noodles
1/4 cup butter
1/4 cup finely chopped parsley

Salt
Freshly ground black pepper

Cook noodles according to package directions. Drain thoroughly. Stir in melted butter, parsley, salt and lots of freshly ground black pepper.

✤

R1

POLENTA BEL PAESE

6 to 8 servings

3 cups boiling water
1 teaspoon salt
1 cup cornmeal
1 cup cold water

12 ounces Bel Paese (or other mild cheese such as Gouda, Colby, Muenster, Monterey Jack), grated
4 tablespoons butter

Bring 3 cups water to a boil. Combine salt, cornmeal and 1 cup cold water and mix well. Pour into boiling water and bring to boil again, stirring. Reduce heat so mixture simmers and cook for 5 minutes, or until cornmeal is thick and water has evaporated.

Turn hot cooked polenta into greased 9-x-9-inch pan and spread to make a layer about ½ inch thick. Chill an hour or two or overnight. Cut into cubes and place in greased shallow baking dish; sprinkle with grated cheese and bits of butter.

Refrigerate, if desired. To serve, return to room temperature and bake at 400 degrees until polenta is hot, bubbly and lightly browned, about 25 to 30 minutes.

✤

F / R1

RAISIN PILAF

10 servings

½ cup plus 2 tablespoons butter
2 large onions, minced
2 cloves garlic, minced
2½ cups brown rice
½ teaspoon cinnamon, heaping

Salt and pepper to taste
5 to 6 cups Chicken Broth (page 90)
¾ cup raisins
5 tablespoons chopped toasted almonds

In 6 tablespoons butter sauté onions and garlic until soft. Stir in rice and cook 5 to 6 minutes. Add cinnamon, salt and pepper and enough chicken broth to cover rice.

Refrigerate or freeze, if desired. To serve, return to room temperature, cover and simmer for 45 to 60 minutes, until rice is tender and liquid has been absorbed. Stir in remaining butter, raisins and almonds; heat and serve.

❦

F / Rl

RICE AND PECAN CASSEROLE

14 to 16 servings

½ pound butter
4 green onions, white part only, chopped
1 clove garlic, minced
1 pound mushrooms, sliced
2 cups brown rice

½ teaspoon dried thyme
¼ teaspoon turmeric
Salt and freshly ground black pepper to taste
1½ cups chopped pecans
6 cups Beef Stock (page 89)

Melt butter. Sauté onions, garlic and mushrooms in butter until onion is golden. Stir in rice and cook, stirring frequently, until rice is golden. Season with thyme, turmeric, salt and pepper. Stir in pecans. Turn into 3-quart casserole and pour over the stock.

If desired, refrigerate or freeze. To serve, return to room temperature and cover. Bake at 400 degrees for 1 hour and 20 minutes, or until liquid is absorbed.

༜

R1

SAUCE VINAIGRETTE FOR HOT ASPARAGUS

8 servings

6 tablespoons olive oil or salad
  oil
2 tablespoons white or red wine
  vinegar

½ to 1 teaspoon salt
12 grinds of pepper mill
1 teaspoon Dijon mustard
4 pounds fresh asparagus

Blend oil and vinegar, salt and pepper. Blend in mustard. Beat with wire whisk. Refrigerate, if desired. To serve, return to room temperature and, just before pouring over asparagus, beat again with wire whisk.

To cook asparagus, break off tough ends, wash and cook over boiling water in a steamer, just until tender. Drain and pour dressing over hot asparagus. Serve immediately.

༜

R1

STUFFED ZUCCHINI

6 servings

6 small zucchini, cut in half
  lengthwise
Olive oil
2 small cloves garlic, minced
⅓ cup bread crumbs

6 black Greek olives, chopped
1 tablespoon capers
1 tablespoon chopped parsley
6 anchovy fillets, coarsely
  chopped

Scoop out and discard seeds and a small amount of flesh from zucchini. Sauté halves quickly in olive oil. Then, in a saucepan, parboil for 5 minutes; cool. Sauté garlic and crumbs in 3 tablespoons oil for 2 minutes. Add chopped olives, capers, parsley and anchovies. Stuff zucchini with this mixture and sprinkle with additional crumbs.

Brush zucchini with oil. Arrange in baking dish and bake at 375 degrees for 20 minutes, or until tender, brushing once with oil. Chill. Serve cold. (May be served hot, as well.)

ᴙ1

SWEET POTATOES AND WALNUTS

10 to 12 servings

3 pounds sweet potatoes
2 tablespoons brown sugar
3 tablespoons butter
½ teaspoon cinnamon
½ teaspoon nutmeg

Salt to taste
1 cup milk
½ cup brandy
1 cup broken walnut meats

Cook sweet potatoes in their jackets. Drop them in boiling water to cover and cook, covered, until tender, about 25 minutes for medium. Drain; cool enough so they can be handled in order to peel. Mash while still warm.

Grease a 2-quart casserole. Combine warm mashed potatoes with remaining ingredients and turn into prepared casserole. Bake at 400 degrees for 30 minutes.

To prepare ahead, refrigerate after combining ingredients in casserole. To serve, return to room temperature and bake at 400 degrees for 30 to 45 minutes.

❦

Rl

TOMATO ZUCCHINI CASSEROLE

6 to 8 servings

Butter
3 medium zucchini, scrubbed
and sliced into ovals on the
diagonal
1 large onion, sliced
3 large tomatoes, sliced
4 anchovy fillets, cut up

1 tablespoon capers
1 clove garlic, minced
1 teaspoon salt
Freshly ground black pepper to
taste
2 teaspoons dried basil
½ cup freshly grated Parmesan
cheese

Rub shallow ovenproof casserole with butter. Line dish with half of sliced zucchini, onion and tomatoes. Top with half of anchovies, capers, garlic, salt, pepper, basil and cheese. Dot with butter. Repeat layers. Dot with butter.

Refrigerate, if desired. To serve, return to room temperature and bake, uncovered, at 375 degrees for 45 minutes, or until zucchini is tender.

❦

Rl

WINTER SQUASH WITH NUTS AND MADEIRA

6 servings

2 acorn squash, or 1 butternut
squash, approximately 1¼
pounds (enough to make 3
cups of ¼-inch-thick slices)
2 tablespoons butter
2 tablespoons oil
1 cup heavy cream

¼ cup Madeira
Salt and freshly ground black
pepper to taste
½ cup bread crumbs
½ cup walnuts or pecans,
coarsely chopped
2 tablespoons melted butter

Peel, quarter and seed squash. Cut into 1/4-inch-thick slices. Sauté the slices in the butter and oil until lightly browned, about 2 to 3 minutes. Butter a 1-quart baking dish. Place half the squash in the dish. Sprinkle with salt and pepper. In a bowl combine the cream and Madeira, and pour half this mixture over the squash in the dish. Top with remaining squash; season and pour over remaining cream mixture. Combine bread crumbs and nuts with melted butter and sprinkle over the top. Bake at 325 degrees for 45 minutes, or until squash is done.

To prepare ahead, refrigerate after casserole is complete. To serve, allow to sit at room temperature for about 30 minutes and then bake as directed for 55 minutes to 60 minutes.

❧

ZUCCHINI WITH WALNUTS

4 servings

1 pound zucchini	1 tablespoon butter
3 tablespoons butter	Salt and freshly ground black
1/2 cup walnuts, coarsely chopped	pepper

Wash zucchini, remove ends and cut into slices 1 inch thick. Heat 3 tablespoons butter in frying pan and sauté zucchini until they just begin to soften.

Meanwhile, brown walnuts in 1 tablespoon butter. Combine the walnuts with the zucchini; season with salt and pepper and cook until zucchini is tender.

Walnuts can be sautéed ahead and set aside.

❧ IX ❧

SALADS

❧

R1

CHINESE SHREDDED CUCUMBER

8 servings

4 cucumbers	5 teaspoons peanut oil
Salt	1 teaspoon sesame oil
1 large clove garlic, minced	1 teaspoon sugar
2 tablespoons light soy sauce	1 teaspoon vinegar

Peel and shred cucumbers, reserving a section for the sliced garnish. Sprinkle well with salt. Let stand 1 to 2 hours and then drain. Combine minced garlic with soy sauce, peanut and sesame oils, sugar and vinegar. Blend well. Add to cucumbers. Toss well and refrigerate, if desired, or serve immediately. If refrigerated, when ready to serve, pour off excessive liquid. Decorate with thinly sliced cucumber.

❧

COOL GREENS

6 servings

½ cup olive oil	5 cups torn spinach
4 tablespoons red wine vinegar	1 small bunch watercress
1 clove garlic, halved	2 avocados
1 tablespoon chopped parsley	2 large oranges, peeled,
1 teaspoon dry mustard	sectioned and cut in half,
1 teaspoon salt	optional
Freshly ground black pepper	½ red onion, thinly sliced, if
5 cups torn lettuce	available

Combine oil, vinegar, garlic, parsley, mustard, salt and pepper; chill. In advance, wash and tear up greens and remove stems from watercress. Refrigerate in plastic bags. At serving time, arrange greens in salad bowl, slice in avocado, optional oranges and onion. Remove garlic from dressing. Shake well and pour over salad. Toss gently.

❧

R2

CRANBERRY SALAD MOLD

8 to 10 servings

2 packages unflavored gelatin	2 oranges, seeded and ground
½ cup cold water	2 cups finely chopped celery
2½ cups orange juice	1 cup chopped walnuts
2 cups ground raw cranberries	½ cup sugar

Soften gelatin in cold water and dissolve over low heat. Remove from heat and stir in orange juice. Chill until partially set. Combine cranberries, oranges, celery and walnuts, and stir in sugar. Add cranberry mixture to the partially set gelatin, and pour into 8-cup mold. Chill until firm. Unmold to serve.

❧

R1

CUCUMBER SALAD

6 to 8 servings

3 to 4 cucumbers	⅓ cup vinegar (white distilled)
1 tablespoon salt	1 or 2 cloves garlic, mashed
1¼ cups water	Sour cream and paprika for
¼ cup sugar	garnish

Peel cucumbers with potato peeler. Slice thinly. In mixing bowl combine salt, water, sugar, vinegar and garlic; mix well. Pour dressing over cucumbers and allow to stand for at least 1 hour in refrigerator before serving. Serve in large salad bowl (not wood) with some of dressing. Garnish with sour cream and paprika.

ᘒ

R1

CUCUMBER WALNUT SALAD

4 servings

8 ounces plain yogurt
1 tablespoon olive oil
1 teaspoon dry white wine
½ teaspoon salt
1 teaspoon chopped fresh dill,
  or ⅓ teaspoon dried dill

1 clove garlic, minced
White pepper to taste
2 large cucumbers, peeled and
  chopped
½ cup walnut pieces

Blend all ingredients but cucumbers and walnuts. When smooth, add cucumbers. Place in refrigerator to chill; overnight, if desired. At last minute stir in walnuts and serve.

ᘒ

ELSA'S GREENS AND MUSHROOM SALAD

6 to 8 servings

Elsa Castro, our housekeeper, makes the best salad in town.

1 pound mixture of Boston lettuce, endive, spinach and red lettuce
¼ pound mushrooms, thinly sliced
¾ to 1 cup coarsely grated Muenster or Cheddar cheese
1 to 1¼ cups Oil and Vinegar Dressing (page 188)

Tear lettuce into bite-size pieces. Mix gently with mushrooms and cheese. Toss with dressing to serve.

❧

R1 (VEGETABLES)
R2 (MARINADE)

FRESH VEGETABLE MARINADE

12 servings

1 tablespoon dry mustard
1 tablespoon sugar
1 tablespoon salt
1 cup cider vinegar
1 teaspoon black pepper
1 cup olive oil ⎫
1 cup salad oil ⎬ or use 2 cups salad oil

1 tablespoon minced parsley
2 pounds small fresh
  mushrooms, cleaned
4 pint baskets small cherry
  tomatoes

Mix together mustard, sugar and salt. Slowly add vinegar until dry mixture is absorbed. Add oil, pepper and parsley, and stir or shake until oil and vinegar are blended. Pour over vegetables. Allow vegetables to marinate overnight. To serve, remove vegetables from marinade.

❧

R1

NECTARINE AND CUCUMBER SALAD

10 servings

2 cups plain yogurt
2 tablespoons chopped fresh
  mint, or 2 teaspoons dried
  mint
1 teaspoon salt

½ teaspoon sugar
1 large clove garlic
2½ pounds nectarines, sliced
2 cucumbers, pared and sliced
  thinly

Combine yogurt, mint, salt, sugar and garlic and mix well. Place a layer of nectarines and then a layer of cucumbers in a shallow serving dish. Spoon on some of the yogurt mixture; repeat this layering, ending with nectarines and topping with yogurt mixture. Cover and refrigerate for at least 2 hours, overnight if desired. Serve with slotted spoon.

❧

ORANGE SPINACH SALAD

6 to 8 servings

10 ounces raw spinach, washed, drained and stems removed
¼ pound mushrooms, sliced

1 (5-ounce) can water chestnuts, drained and diced
4 oranges, peeled and diced

R1
Dressing:

¼ cup salad oil
2 tablespoons vinegar
2 tablespoons orange juice

1 tablespoon soy sauce
¼ teaspoon salt
¼ teaspoon dry mustard

Tear spinach coarsely and toss in large salad bowl with mushrooms, water chestnuts and oranges. Combine dressing ingredients thoroughly and toss with spinach mixture just before serving.

Salad dressing can be made a day ahead.

❧

R3

PICKLED BEETS

Makes approximately 4 cups

2 pounds beets
1 cup wine vinegar
1 teaspoon salt
Pinch of sugar

5 peppercorns
4 whole cloves
½ bay leaf

Cut off tops from beets, leaving 1-inch stem. Wash. Place beets in boiling water to half-cover them. Cover and cook about 45 minutes, until tender but still firm. If necessary, add more boiling water. Drain beets, reserving 1 cup of beet liquid.

Plunge beets into cold water to stop cooking process. Drain; peel off skins and cut into slices. Place in container with tight cover. Combine reserved beet liquid with remaining ingredients in pot and bring to boil. Pour over beets; be sure they are completely covered. Cover and chill. Serve drained and chilled.

NOTE: Pickled Beets should be made several days in advance. They are a fine accompaniment to the Koulibiac (page 112).

℘

R1

PIQUANT ZUCCHINI

8 servings

4 medium zucchini, trimmed and scrubbed	¼ teaspoon thyme
	1 teaspoon coriander
¼ cup olive oil	1 bay leaf
¼ cup lemon juice	1 clove garlic, crushed
1 teaspoon salt	2 tablespoons chopped parsley
¼ teaspoon pepper	

Slice zucchini ¼ inch thick. Combine all other ingredients in saucepan. Add zucchini. Bring to boiling. Reduce heat; simmer until zucchini is tender, about 5 to 7 minutes. Chill.

✌

R1
POTATO SALAD

6 to 8 servings

4 cups cooked potatoes, cubed
1 small onion, minced
1 tablespoon minced fresh
  parsley
Salt and pepper to taste
1 teaspoon capers, drained
1½ teaspoons chopped fresh dill,
  or ½ teaspoon dillweed

1 egg
5 teaspoons lemon juice
1½ tablespoons wine vinegar
2 hard-cooked eggs, diced
¾ cup sour cream
¼ cup Mayonnaise (page 42)
¼ cup celery, chopped
¼ cup green pepper, chopped

In large bowl mix potatoes with onion, parsley, salt, pepper, capers and dill. Beat egg with lemon juice and vinegar; mix in diced eggs, sour cream, mayonnaise, celery and green pepper. Add to potato mixture; chill and serve.

✌

RED AND GREEN SALAD

6 servings

3 tablespoons olive oil
2 tablespoons red wine vinegar
1½ tablespoons Dijon-style
  mustard
Salt and freshly ground black
  pepper to taste
1 large clove garlic, pressed

¼ small head red cabbage,
  coarsely shredded
10 raw Brussels sprouts, very
  thinly sliced
⅓ cup blue cheese, crumbled
2 tablespoons chopped green
  onion

Mix together oil, vinegar, mustard, salt, pepper and garlic. Beat or shake to blend well. (Dressing can be made ahead.) Gently stir dressing into cabbage and Brussels sprouts just before serving, along with cheese and green onion.

R1

ROASTED PEPPER AND MUSHROOM SALAD

5 or 6 servings

5 green peppers
1 pound mushrooms, washed, stems removed

½ cup Oil and Vinegar Dressing (page 188)
Salt and freshly ground black pepper to taste

Roast peppers at 450 degrees for 15 to 20 minutes, until skins blister and brown. Cool; remove skin. Remove stems and seeds, and slice into ¼-inch-thick strips.

Slice mushroom caps; reserve stems for another use. Combine peppers and mushrooms and toss with dressing. Season with salt and pepper as needed. Chill.

R2

SEAFOAM SALAD

6 to 8 servings

1-pound, 4-ounce can unsweetened crushed pineapple
2 packages unflavored gelatin
1 cup water
4 tablespoons lime juice

4 tablespoons sugar
¼ teaspoon salt
1 teaspoon dillweed
½ cup dry vermouth
2 cups unflavored yogurt

Drain pineapple well, reserving juices. Add juices to gelatin with water, lime juice, sugar, salt and dill. Mix well and heat to boiling, stirring to dissolve gelatin. Remove from heat and stir in vermouth. Chill until mixture is consistency of unbeaten egg white. Blend in yogurt. Stir in pineapple. Pour into 1½-quart ring or other shaped mold and chill until firm. Unmold to serve.

ও

SPINACH SALAD WITH YOGURT DRESSING

6 servings

2 pounds fresh spinach
3 hard-cooked eggs, coarsely chopped

8 slices crisply cooked and well-drained nitrite-free bacon, crumbled
⅔ cup Yogurt Dressing (page 189)

Wash spinach well and dry thoroughly by draining on racks or in colander. Break into bite-size pieces and mix gently with eggs and bacon. Toss with dressing just before serving.

ও

R2

TANGY RICE SALAD

4 to 6 servings

4 cups fluffy cooked rice
1 tablespoon vinegar
1 teaspoon lemon juice
1 tablespoon salad oil
2 teaspoons Curry Powder or more to taste (page 39)

¼ teaspoon turmeric
¾ cup raisins
⅓ cup chopped green pepper
⅔ cup yogurt or sour cream
⅔ cup Mayonnaise (page 42)

Sprinkle hot rice with vinegar, lemon juice and oil. Mix lightly; add curry and turmeric, and blend. Stir in raisins and green pepper. Add the yogurt and mayonnaise; mix well. Place in 6-cup mold and chill. Either unmold to serve or heap on lettuce-lined plate.

❧

R1

WHITE BEAN AND TUNA SALAD
(*FAGIOLI TOSCANI ALL' OLIO*)

6 servings

2 cups dry white kidney, marrow, Great Northern, or navy beans
2 quarts water
¼ cup olive oil
1 tablespoon lemon juice
Salt and lots of freshly ground pepper

¼ cup green onions, finely chopped
2 tablespoons parsley, finely chopped
1 (7-ounce) can tuna, preferably packed in olive oil

Combine beans with water and bring to boil. Boil briskly for 2 minutes, remove from heat and let beans soak 1 hour. Then cook them in soaking water over low heat for another 1½ hours, or until tender. Add more water if necessary. Drain.

Combine oil, lemon juice, salt and pepper, and pour over beans. Add green onions and parsley, and mix gently. Refrigerate. To serve, drain tuna, break into chunks and place on top of beans.

☙

ʀ1

WINTER SALAD

12 servings

4 large Bermuda or Spanish onions, sliced	½ teaspoon pepper
2 cups milk	1 teaspoon sugar
2 cups water	½ cup olive or salad oil
4 hard-cooked eggs, chopped	4 tablespoons cider vinegar
2 teaspoons prepared mustard	2 small bunches celery, diced
2 teaspoons salt	4 large beets, cooked, peeled and sliced

Boil onion slices in milk and water until tender. Drain and chill onions.

To make the dressing, chop eggs and mix with mustard, salt, pepper and sugar. Stir in oil, blending well. Then stir in vinegar.

Toss the onions with celery and beets; spoon dressing over and mix gently. Let stand for several hours in the refrigerator.

☙

ʀ1

ZUCCHINI SALAD

6 servings

6 small zucchini, scrubbed, ends cut off	Lettuce
1 tablespoon salt	Oil and Vinegar Dressing (page 188)

Cook zucchini in salt water until almost tender, about 5 minutes; drain. When cool, slice thinly lengthwise in about ⅓-inch-thick slices to within 1 inch of bottom, but not through skin. Refrigerate. When ready to serve, spread each zucchini out in a fan shape on lettuce-lined plate. Pour dressing over.

ꙮ

Rl

LEMON AND OIL DRESSING

Makes 1 cup

1 small clove garlic, cut in half
¼ teaspoon dry mustard
6 tablespoons olive oil

2 tablespoons fresh lemon juice
Salt and freshly ground black
   pepper to taste

In a bowl combine all ingredients and blend with a fork or wire whisk. Refrigerate. To serve, shake dressing well, remove garlic and pour over greens.

ꙮ

Rl

OIL AND VINEGAR DRESSING

Makes approximately 1⅓ cups

⅓ cup-plus wine vinegar
1 teaspoon salt
⅛ teaspoon pepper
½ teaspoon sugar

¼ teaspoon paprika
½ teaspoon dry mustard
1 cup olive or salad oil
1 clove garlic

Mix the vinegar with the seasonings and add the oil slowly while beating.

༏

R3

ROQUEFORT SOUR CREAM DRESSING

Makes approximately 1¼ cups

1 cup sour cream
½ teaspoon dry mustard
½ teaspoon minced onion

2 ounces Roquefort or other
good blue cheese, crumbled
2 tablespoons dry white wine

Combine all ingredients and mix well. Use for sliced tomatoes or on any kind of salad, such as green or tossed.

༏

R2

YOGURT DRESSING

Makes 1 cup

1 cup plain yogurt
1 teaspoon lemon juice
½ teaspoon minced chives
½ teaspoon dry mustard

¼ teaspoon paprika
Salt and pepper to taste
1 small clove garlic, mashed

Combine ingredients thoroughly and chill. Allow to sit at least several hours for flavors to blend.

X

BREADS

F / Rl

BRIOCHE

1 package yeast
¼ cup lukewarm water
2 cups flour
3 eggs plus 1 egg yolk

¾ cup sweet butter
½ teaspoon salt
1 tablespoon sugar

Dissolve the yeast in lukewarm water. Stir in ½ cup flour until it forms a stiff ball. Turn out on lightly floured surface and knead a little to get a smooth surface. Cut a cross on the top of the ball and drop into a pitcher of lukewarm water. Let ball rise to the top (it will take 5 to 7 minutes).

Spoon 1½ cups flour onto pastry board. Make a well in the center and break in 2 eggs. Begin to knead the paste, adding the third egg little by little, to make a soft dough. Then pick up and crash down onto board about 100 times. The dough will be elastic when it detaches itself cleanly from fingers.

Knead the butter with the salt and sugar and then knead it into the dough. Mix it thoroughly but gently. Be sure not to overwork dough or it will lose its elasticity. Remove ball of sponge from water and drain on towel. Add it to dough, cutting and folding in. Form into ball and put it in floured bowl. Cover with plastic wrap and damp towel. Let it rise in warm place until double in bulk, about 2 hours. Turn the dough out onto lightly floured board and punch down. Return to bowl and chill for 6 hours, or overnight. It will rise a little. Punch down and proceed.

For individual brioches (about 8 to 10):

Place dough on lightly floured surface. Shape two-thirds of it into 2-inch balls to fit into 3-inch fluted brioche molds or muffin tins. Form an equal number of "hats," shaped something like a pear. Cut a cross in the base or make a depression and fit hat into depression. Be sure the base does not fill the mold more than half full. Cover and let rise about 30 minutes or until double in bulk. Cut around the base of the hat to keep it separate from the body during baking. Brush surface of brioche with a mixture of the egg yolk and 1 tablespoon water. Bake at 425 degrees for 15 to 20 minutes, until golden.

For one large brioche:

Fill fluted brioche mold half full and make hat with remaining dough, following procedure above.

Bake at 425 degrees for about 30 minutes, until golden.

For miniatures:

Use the smallest-size brioche molds; follow directions above and bake at 425 degrees for 7 to 10 minutes. Cool. To use for hors d'oeuvres, remove hats; hollow out brioche and dry the shell at 350 degrees for 3 to 4 minutes. Fill as desired and replace hats. Heat before serving. (Eat the insides!)

ॐ

F / R1

CARROT BREAD

2 loaves

4 eggs	¼ teaspoon salt
¾ cup honey	2 teaspoons cinnamon
½ cup unsulfured molasses	½ teaspoon cloves
1¼ cups salad oil	½ teaspoon nutmeg
2½ cups whole-wheat flour	2 teaspoons grated orange
2 teaspoons baking powder	peel
1½ teaspoons baking soda	2 cups grated carrots

Beat eggs in large bowl; add honey and molasses gradually and beat until thoroughly mixed. Add oil slowly and continue beating until well mixed. Stir in flour, baking powder, baking soda, salt, cinnamon, cloves, nutmeg and orange peel. Blend until mixture is smooth and stir in carrots.

Pour batter into 2 greased 9-x-5-inch loaf pans and bake at 350 degrees for 30 minutes. Reduce heat to 300 degrees and bake about 20 minutes longer, or until loaves test done. Tester should come out clean when stuck in center of bread. Cool in pans 10 minutes. Place loaves on wire racks and cool completely. Wrap in aluminum foil and store overnight before serving, or freeze. When loaves defrost, they will have mellowed.

F / R1

CHEESE AND APPLE BREAD

1 loaf

This tastes best the second day.

½ cup butter	½ teaspoon baking soda
2 eggs	1 teaspoon salt
⅔ cup sugar	1 cup peeled shredded apples
2 cups flour	½ cup shredded Cheddar cheese
1½ teaspoons baking powder	

Combine butter, eggs and dry ingredients in large mixing bowl; blend well. Stir in apples and cheese. Turn into well-greased 9-x-5-inch loaf pan. Bake at 350 degrees, about 50 to 60 minutes, until center of loaf tests done. Cool thoroughly before removing from pan. Serve with sweet butter.

Freeze, if desired.

♾

F / R3

GEORGIAN BREAD

Approximately 24 pieces

2 packages fresh yeast
1 tablespoon plus ½ teaspoon
  sugar
1 cup warm milk

3½ cups flour, approximately
  (more may be needed)
2 teaspoons salt
¼ pound butter, softened

Cheese filling:

1¼ pounds Muenster cheese,
  grated

2 tablespoons butter,
  softened
2 eggs

Sprinkle yeast and ½ teaspoon sugar over ½ cup warm milk. Allow to stand 2 to 3 minutes; then stir to dissolve yeast.

In warm place allow yeast to double in volume, about 8 minutes. Place flour in large bowl. Make well in center; add remaining milk, yeast mixture, 1 tablespoon sugar, salt and butter. With large spoon, blend in flour with other ingredients until too thick to stir. Then, using fingers, blend to form dough. Add more flour, if needed, to gather into ball. Knead dough on lightly floured surface for 6 to 10 minutes, until it is elastic, sprinkling on more flour as needed to keep the dough from sticking. Form into ball and place in lightly oiled bowl. Cover and allow to rise in warm place about 45 minutes, or until doubled in bulk. Punch dough down and allow to rise again for 30 minutes, until doubled in bulk again.

While dough is rising, prepare cheese filling. Combine cheese, butter and 1 egg in large bowl and beat with spoon until well blended and smooth.

Punch dough down and roll out on lightly floured board to thickness of about ⅟₁₆ inch. Cut into 4½-inch circles. On each round of dough, spread 1½ tablespoons cheese, leaving about 1½-inch border uncovered. Draw edges of dough up over filling to center, covering it and forming 6 pleats to make a hexagon-shaped pastry, or fold over sides and then fold in edges. Arrange on greased baking sheets; brush tops with remaining egg, which has been lightly beaten. Allow dough to rest 10 minutes, then bake at 375 degrees for 20 to 25 minutes, or until golden-brown. Serve warm.

These can be prepared several days ahead, refrigerated, and reheated at 350 degrees for 10 to 15 minutes. They can be prepared further in advance and frozen. To serve, defrost and reheat.

❦

F

MIKE'S BREAD

4 loaves

My son, Michael, decided to contribute an original bread recipe to the book. Since he spent one summer baking bread for a living, he's well qualified to innovate. This crunchy-crusted, spongy-textured loaf with nutlike flavor was an instant success.

1 cup cornmeal, uncooked	2 tablespoons yeast
1 cup whole-wheat cereal, uncooked	½ cup honey
	2 teaspoons salt
1 cup regular oatmeal, uncooked	2 cups whole-wheat flour
	6 to 8 cups unbleached flour

Heat 4 cups of water to boiling. Pour boiling water over cornmeal, wheat cereal and oatmeal; cool. Meanwhile, add yeast to 1 cup warm water, and "proof." The yeast is proofed when small bubbles appear on the surface, in about 5 to 7 minutes. When water-grain mixture is cooled to about 100 degrees or so, add yeast mixture to it. Then add honey, 1 cup water and salt. Stir well. Add whole-wheat flour, ½ cup at a time, mixing well with spoon between additions. Add unbleached flour, about 1 cup at a time, mixing with spoon. When dough becomes too stiff to mix with spoon, use hands. Use only enough of the unbleached flour to make a soft dough which will still be sticky.

Turn out on well-floured board and knead for 5 minutes. Dough will still be sticky. Place in well-greased bowl, cover with damp cloth and place in warm place to rise until doubled in bulk, or until a finger pressed into dough leaves imprint, about 1 hour.

Punch dough down; turn out on lightly floured board. Shape into 4 loaves and place in well-greased 9-x-5-inch loaf pans. Cover with wax paper and allow to rise in warm place until doubled in bulk, about 1 hour.

Bake at 350 degrees for about 65 minutes, or until loaves test done. Remove from pans and cool on wire racks before slicing.

❧

ONION POPOVERS

6 large popovers

3 eggs
1 cup milk
3 tablespoons chopped onion
¼ teaspoon salt

1 tablespoon melted shortening or oil
1 cup sifted flour

Blend together eggs, milk, onion, salt and shortening. Blend in flour until smooth, then beat at least 1 minute in electric mixer or 3 minutes with rotary beater. Fill well-greased custard cups half full. Bake at 400 degrees for 40 to 45 minutes, or until dark golden-brown and firm to the touch. Serve immediately.

❧

F / R1

PORTUGUESE SWEET BREAD

2 round loaves

2 packages yeast
¼ cup warm water·
1 cup sugar
6 to 7 cups flour, approximately
1 teaspoon salt

1 cup milk, scalded and cooled to room temperature
3 eggs, room temperature
¼ pound sweet butter
1 beaten egg for glaze

In small bowl dissolve yeast in warm water. In large mixing bowl combine sugar, 4 cups flour and salt. Make a well in center of flour mixture and pour in yeast and milk. Add eggs and stir mixture until ingredients are combined. Beat in small pieces of butter. Then add more flour until dough forms soft ball. When it become difficult to stir the dough, work in flour with fingers. Turn dough out onto floured board and knead it with the heel of your hand until it is smooth and elastic.

Grease bowl and place dough in it. Cover and place in warm place to rise until double in bulk, about 1 hour. Dough is ready when a dent remains in it after it has been poked with a finger. Punch dough down; divide in half and let rest for 10 minutes.

Grease two 9-inch pie plates. Pat each half of dough into 8-inch round in each plate. Cover and place in warm place to rise again until doubled in bulk, about 40 minutes.

Brush top of each loaf with beaten egg and bake at 350 degrees for 45 to 60 minutes. Loaves are done when wooden toothpick inserted in center comes out clean. If tops brown too much before loaves are baked, cover tops lightly with aluminum foil. Cool loaves on wire rack. Serve warm with sweet butter.

Loaves freeze beautifully.

ಲ್ಲಿ

SOPAIPILLAS

Approximately 20

The *sopaipillas* can be served just as a hot bread with soup or *guacamole*. In New Mexico they are always served with the meal, but with sweet toppings.

1¾ cups flour	2 tablespoons shortening
2 teaspoons baking powder	⅔ cup cold water
1 teaspoon salt	Oil for deep-fat frying

Sift together dry ingredients; add shortening and cut in with pastry blender or knives. Gradually add just enough cold water to make dough of pastry consistency. Turn out on lightly floured board and knead gently until smooth. Cover dough and let rest for 5 minutes.

Roll out into even, 12-x-15-inch rectangle, about ⅛ to ¹⁄₁₆ inch thick. Cut into 2-x-3-inch pieces or 3-inch squares.

Cover dough with wax paper. Heat oil in deep pan to 375 degrees. Drop dough into very hot oil, a few at a time, turning them over 3 or 4 times so that they will puff evenly.

Allow to turn golden-brown on both sides. Serve warm with confectioners' sugar, warm honey or warm apple jelly.

ಆ

F / R1

STEPHANIE HARRIS'S OATMEAL-PLUS BREAD

3 loaves

Stephanie Harris, a vegetarian, puts lots of protein into this bread. It is not exactly simple, but it makes a wonderfully crunchy, thick, heavy loaf.

4½ cups water	¾ cup warm water
2 cups rolled oats, uncooked	¾ cup soy flour
1 cup high-protein cereal, uncooked *	4 cups whole-wheat flour
	1 cup triticale flour
½ cup 12-grain cereal (or high-protein cereal) *, uncooked	4 cups unbleached white flour
	¼ cup wheat germ
4½ teaspoons salt	½ cup nonfat-milk powder
½ cup honey	250-milligram vitamin C tablet,
3 tablespoons margarine	crushed, mixed with 5
3 tablespoons yeast (3 cakes)	teaspoons whole-wheat flour

Combine water, cereals and salt, and boil for 1 minute. Stir in honey and margarine. While cooling, dissolve yeast in warm water. Then add

---

* These high-protein cereals are available in many natural-food stores. If only one kind is available, use 1½ cups of it.

to cooled cereal. Sift flours and add to cereals. Add milk powder and wheat germ. Crush vitamin C tablet; mix with whole-wheat flour and add 4½ teaspoons of mixture to dough. Turn out onto floured board and knead until smooth. Put in greased bowl and let rise until double in bulk, covered with damp towel. Knead again briefly and divide into 3 loaves. Place in greased 9-x-5-inch pans and let rise, covered, until doubled in bulk. Bake at 375 degrees for 40 minutes, or until well browned. Loaves freeze well.

❧

WARM SPRINGS INDIAN FRIED BREAD

6 to 8 cakes

This recipe is from the Warm Springs Indian reservation in Oregon. Serve the bread with lots of butter.

3 cups sifted flour
2 teaspoons baking powder
1 teaspoon salt
1 teaspoon sugar

1 tablespoon butter
¾ to 1 cup warm milk
Fat for deep frying

Combine dry ingredients; cut in butter. Add enough warm milk to make a dough that is soft but easy to handle. Knead on floured board until dough is very smooth, soft but elastic. Don't use a lot of extra flour. Divide dough into 6 or 8 balls, each about the size of a lemon. Brush tops with melted butter. Cover and let stand 30 to 45 minutes.

Pat out each ball into a round 5 or 6 inches in diameter and ¼ inch thick. Fry in deep hot fat which has been heated to 365 degrees. Dough should rise to surface immediately. Cook until brown on one side; turn and brown on other side. Be careful not to pierce crust of bread in turning. Drain thoroughly on absorbent paper.

❧

F / R1

WHOLE-WHEAT BANANA BREAD

2 loaves

1⅓ cups honey
1 cup unsalted butter
3 large, very ripe bananas, mashed
4 eggs
3 cups whole-wheat flour

1 tablespoon baking powder
½ teaspoon salt
1 teaspoon nutmeg
½ cup milk
1 teaspoon vanilla

Cream honey and butter; add mashed bananas and beat well. Add eggs. Combine dry ingredients and add to batter alternately with milk, and then add vanilla. Spoon into 2 greased 9-x-5-inch loaf pans and bake at 350 degrees for 50 to 55 minutes. Cool in pans on rack for 10 minutes; remove from pans and cool completely on rack.

The bread should not be served until it has been allowed to mellow for 1 day, well wrapped in foil and left at room temperature. Alternately, the bread may be frozen; it will be ready to eat after defrosting.

❧

F / R3

ZUCCHINI WALNUT BREAD

2 loaves

2½ cups shredded, unpeeled zucchini
1 cup whole-wheat flour
1½ cups unbleached flour
2 teaspoons baking powder
½ teaspoon baking soda
1 teaspoon cinnamon
½ teaspoon nutmeg
½ teaspoon ground cloves

¾ teaspoon salt
3 eggs
1¼ cups sugar
¾ cup vegetable oil
¼ cup honey
½ cup raisins
2 teaspoons grated lemon rind
1 cup chopped walnuts

Shred zucchini and allow to sit in strainer to allow moisture to drain off. Stir together flours, baking powder, baking soda, spices and salt. Beat eggs until very light. Gradually beat in sugar, beating until mixture is light. Beat in oil until mixture is light. Blend in flour mixture with rubber spatula until smooth. Add zucchini, honey, raisins, lemon rind and nuts. Stir until well mixed. Spoon batter into 2 greased 9-x-5-inch loaf pans and bake at 350 degrees for 40 to 50 minutes, until loaves are done. Cool in pan 10 minutes. Then remove and cool on wire racks. Wrap in aluminum foil and store overnight before slicing.

Freeze, if desired.

❧ XI ❧

DESSERTS

FRUIT AND CHEESE

Apples—with Camembert, Cheddar, blues, Parmesan
Bananas—with goat cheeses such as *chabichou*
Cantaloupe—with Parmesan
Cherries—with Crema Danica
Figs—with Stilton
Grapes—with Camembert; provolone; feta or other sheep cheese;
    Pont l'Évêque; Appenzeller
Honeydew—with Edam
Nectarines—with Brie
Oranges—with Gorgonzola
Peaches—with triple creams such as Crema Danica, Gervais, Chantilly;
    Gorgonzola
Pears—with Camembert, provolone, blues
Pineapple—with Camembert
Plums—purple with Stilton; red with Appenzeller
Strawberries—with triple creams

R1

CHOCOLATE-DIPPED FRUITS

8 servings

36 to 40 orange segments, or 48 medium-sized strawberries with stems;
   or combination of both
2 (1-pound) packages semisweet chocolate squares

Wash berries and dry. Melt chocolate over hot water to a temperature of about 100 degrees. Stir occasionally. Keep over hot water, but not on the stove while dipping.

If dipping berries, hold them by the stem and swirl around in chocolate. If a berry is without a stem, use a toothpick. Use toothpicks to hold orange segments while dipping. Place dipped fruit on baking sheet which has been covered with wax paper. Cover any spots on the fruit which were missed with a little chocolate on a spoon. Chill dipped fruits until chocolate hardens and serve.

ॐ

Rl

CHOCOLATE-WRAPPED PEARS

6 servings

1 cup sugar	6 firm, ripe pears with stems
4 cups water	4 ounces semisweet chocolate
Juice of 1 lemon	squares
2 cinnamon sticks	4 tablespoons sweet butter,
4 whole cloves	softened
2 tablespoons crème de menthe	Fresh or crystallized mint

Dissolve sugar in water. Add lemon juice, spices and crème de menthe and simmer, tightly covered, for 10 to 15 minutes. Peel the pears carefully, leaving stems intact, and cut a slice off bottoms so they will stand upright. Poach pears in gently boiling syrup until tender, 30 to 40 minutes. Cool pears in syrup and chill thoroughly, overnight.

Melt chocolate in a bowl over warm water. Add butter and stir until it is melted and mixture is smooth. Remove pears from syrup and dry carefully with paper towel. Dip pears in melted chocolate to coat evenly. Use spoon, if necessary, to fill in uncoated spots. Lift pears to drain off excess chocolate; arrange on a serving dish. Decorate top of each pear with sprig of fresh or crytallized mint. Chill until ready to serve.

R1

GRAPES IN BRANDY

4 servings

¾ cup honey
6 tablespoons good brandy
1 tablespoon lemon juice

1 pound seedless grapes,
  washed and drained
1 cup sour cream

Mix the honey, brandy and lemon juice thoroughly. Add the grapes to the mixture and stir gently to coat grapes completely. Chill for several hours, or overnight. Stir occasionally.

To serve, spoon into 4 individual serving dishes and top each portion with ¼ cup sour cream.

MARINATED FRUIT

8 servings

⅔ cup dry vermouth or orange
  juice
5 tablespoons sugar*
½ teaspoon cinnamon

1 large pineapple, cut in wedges
4 navel oranges, peeled and
  sectioned
2 pears, unpeeled and diced

Combine the vermouth, sugar and cinnamon and allow to stand in the refrigerator for at least 1 hour. Strain the liquid, discarding the sugar residue. Pour liquid over prepared fruits. Marinate at least 1 hour in the refrigerator before serving.

---

* If orange juice is used, reduce sugar to 2 tablespoons.

❧

R2

BLUEBERRY KIR SAUCE

5 servings

1 tablespoon butter
1 tablespoon cornstarch
¼ cup crème de cassis
¾ cup dry white wine

1 tablespoon lemon juice
1½ cups fresh or frozen
  blueberries

Melt butter in saucepan. Combine cornstarch and cassis to make a smooth mixture. Gradually stir cassis mixture into melted butter. Add wine and lemon juice and cook, stirring, until mixture is thick. Stir in berries and cook just until they begin to burst. Chill. Serve over vanilla ice cream.

❧

R3

SAUCE FOR NECTARINES (OR PEACHES)

Makes approximately 2 cups

1½ cups sour cream
4½ tablespoons crème de cacao

4½ tablespoons Seville orange
  marmalade
Dash salt

Combine ingredients and serve with chilled, sliced nectarines (or peaches).

Makes enough for 10 to 12 pieces of fruit.

ᔥ

R1

NECTARINES AND BRANDY

4 to 6 servings

6 medium nectarines
¾ cup sugar
1 cup water
3 tablespoons brandy

1½ teaspoons vanilla
1 cup sour cream
1 tablespoon confectioners'
  sugar
2 tablespoons brandy

Blanch and peel nectarines; pit and cut into quarters. In large saucepan, combine nectarines, granulated sugar and water. Bring to boil; simmer 1 minute. Stir in 3 tablespoons brandy and vanilla. Let stand until mixture reaches room temperature; then chill. Just before serving, arrange fruit in 4 to 6 individual dishes. Combine sour cream, confectioners' sugar and remaining brandy; spoon over nectarines and serve.

ᔥ

R1

ORANGES MARINATED IN LIQUEUR

4 servings

6 seedless oranges

12 tablespoons orange liqueur
  or crème de cacao

Peel oranges, removing all of white membrane.* Slice. Place oranges in individual serving dishes or one large serving dish and pour over

---

* To peel oranges easily, plunge them into boiling water and reduce heat to bare simmer. Allow oranges to heat for 3 to 4 minutes. This makes the peel easy to remove and takes most of the white pith with the skin.

I have never found out, however, if the heat destroys a lot of the vitamin C, so I recommend it only when there are a lot of oranges to be peeled for a party.

either orange liqueur or crème de cacao. Refrigerate for 12 to 24
hours, turning oranges occasionally so they are covered with the
liqueur.

Serve chilled.

ॐ

ORANGE ICES

6 servings

2 teaspoons freshly grated
lemon peel
2 tablespoons freshly
squeezed lemon juice
½ pint heavy cream, whipped

1 quart orange sherbet,
softened
¾ cup chilled dry sherry
Fruit or mint leaves for garnish

Have peel and juice prepared ahead. Whip cream.

Place sherbet in bowl with lemon peel and juice. Beat until creamy
while gradually adding chilled sherry. Pour or spoon immediately
into stemmed chilled glasses. Top with whipped cream and garnish
as desired. Serve with straws.

ॐ

Rl

PEACHES IN ORANGE LIQUEUR

6 servings

2 pounds fresh peaches
¼ cup butter
1 cup sugar

½ cup orange liqueur
(Cointreau, Triple Sec or
Grand Marnier)
¼ cup lemon juice
½ cup slivered almonds

Wash, halve and pit peaches. Arrange, cut side down, one layer deep, in shallow baking pan. Cream together butter and sugar; stir in orange liqueur and lemon juice. Spoon mixture over peaches and refrigerate, if desired. To serve, return to room temperature and sprinkle with almonds. Bake at 375 degrees for 35 to 40 minutes, until peaches are soft. Baste with juices once or twice. Serve warm, not hot.

ꙮ

PEARS IN ZABAGLIONE

8 servings

8 firm, ripe pears with stems	¼ to 1 cup sugar, depending
1 lemon, sliced	on ripeness of pears
	Zabaglione Sauce (recipe below)

Peel pears and cut off slice at bottom so they will stand up. In water just to cover the pears, with lemon slices and sugar, cook the pears until tender. Keep water at a simmer; *do not boil.* Drain and chill pears in refrigerator for several hours, or overnight.

Zabaglione Sauce:

8 egg yolks	1 cup Marsala wine
¼ cup sugar	2 tablespoons brandy
	1 tablespoon water

Combine yolks with sugar in top of double boiler. Beat well with rotary beater or wire whisk. Add wine, brandy and water and beat well. Place over hot water and continue beating until mixture thickens. Remove from heat and chill.

To serve, place pears in stemmed goblets or individual glass serving dishes, if possible. Spoon over sauce and decorate with green leaf at stems.

🙣

R1

PEARS WITH GORGONZOLA

6 servings

3 pears, ripe but not mushy   5 ounces Gorgonzola cheese,
softened

Wash pears, halve and remove centers with teaspoon. Also remove woody part, but leave stems intact. Into cavities, spoon the cheese. Refrigerate. It's best to serve the pears when the refrigerator chill is off, so leave them out about 15 minutes before serving.

🙣

R2

RED PLUM COMPOTE

6 servings

⅔ cup sugar   3-inch stick cinnamon
1 cup dry white wine   Zest of ½ lemon
1 cup water   18 firm, ripe, red plums,
4 whole cloves   stemmed and rinsed

Combine sugar, wine, water, cloves, cinnamon and lemon in saucepan large enough to hold the plums. Bring ingredients to boil and cook, uncovered, for 5 minutes.

Add plums and bring mixture to boil; lower heat and simmer the plums 10 to 20 minutes, depending on their ripeness, until they are tender but still hold their shape.

Some plums will be ready before others. Remove them as they are. Then, when all are cooked, return all the plums to the syrup and cool. Chill plums in syrup.

This is excellent served either plain or over vanilla ice cream.

ᵍ

PREPARE-AHEAD CHOCOLATE SOUFFLÉ

8 servings

This is not as light as a traditional French soufflé and, because of the flour content, it can be prepared several hours ahead and baked when it is time to serve.

5 egg yolks	2 ounces unsweetened
¾ cup. sugar	chocolate, melted
4 drops vanilla	8 egg whites
1 cup unbleached flour	Confectioners' sugar
2 cups milk	½ pint heavy cream, whipped

In a bowl beat yolks with ½ cup sugar and vanilla until light and fluffy. Gradually beat in flour until a paste is formed. Meanwhile, bring milk to a boil. Add egg mixture all at once and bring again to boil, beating vigorously with wire whisk until paste is smooth. Continue stirring with wooden spoon until mixture is thick, like a pastry cream. Add melted chocolate and stir until blended. Cool. Beat egg whites until soft peaks form; gradually beat in remaining ¼ cup sugar until stiff peaks form. Fold egg whites into batter. Cover bowl lightly and allow to sit at room temperature for up to 4 hours before serving. To serve, spoon into 8 greased individual 2-inch soufflé dishes and bake at 350 degrees for 20 minutes. Dust with confectioners' sugar and serve with whipped cream on the side.

ᵍ

ʀ1

COLD LEMON SOUFFLÉ

10 to 12 servings

2 envelopes unflavored gelatin	2 cups sugar
½ cup cold water	2 teaspoons grated lemon rind
8 eggs, separated	2 cups heavy cream
1 cup fresh lemon juice	Strawberries and toasted,
1 teaspoon salt	slivered almonds for garnish

To make a collar for the soufflé dish, fold a 30-inch length of foil, 12 inches wide, in half lengthwise. Lightly butter inside of collar and wrap around outside of 2-quart soufflé dish so the collar stands above the rim by 3 inches. Fasten with tape.

Sprinkle gelatin over cold water to soften. In top of double boiler combine yolks, lemon juice, salt and 1 cup sugar. Cook over boiling water, stirring, until mixture coats the back of a spoon. Stir in gelatin and lemon rind; turn into a bowl and refrigerate until mixture is slightly thickened, stirring occasionally.

Beat whites until they hold their shape; gradually beat in 1 cup sugar; continue beating until mixture holds stiff peaks. Whip cream until stiff. Fold cream and whites gently into lemon mixture. Pour into prepared soufflé dish; refrigerate until firm, at least 3 hours.

To serve, remove soufflé collar; top with strawberries and almonds.

ᔕ

R1

ESPRESSO MOUSSE

12 to 15 servings

1 envelope unflavored gelatin	3 tablespoons brandy
¼ cup cold water	1 teaspoon grated lemon peel
1 cup brewed extra-strength espresso coffee	½ cup chopped toasted almonds or chopped walnuts
1 cup sugar	3 egg whites
2 cups heavy cream	¼ teaspoon salt

Sprinkle gelatin over ¼ cup cold water to soften. Heat the coffee and ¾ cup sugar in pan until sugar dissolves. Add gelatin to hot mixture and stir to dissolve gelatin; cool. Pour this mixture into a shallow dish which can go into the freezer. Freeze for 45 minutes or until mixture is solid 1 inch around edge, no more. Pour mixture into cold bowl; beat until smooth and creamy. Whip cream until soft peaks form; fold into coffee mixture with brandy, lemon peel and nuts. Beat egg whites with salt until foamy. Gradually beat in remaining 1/4 cup sugar, beating until stiff peaks form. Fold into coffee mixture. Spoon into 2- or 2½-quart soufflé or similar serving dish and refrigerate for several hours or overnight, until firm.

F

FROZEN GRAND MARNIER SOUFFLÉ

8 servings

2 tablespoons unflavored gelatin, soaked in 1/4 cup water	1⅓ cups orange juice
	2 cups sugar
	⅔ cup Grand Marnier
½ cup boiling water	1 pint heavy cream, whipped
6 egg yolks	Praline

Dissolve gelatin in boiling water. In a separate bowl beat egg yolks until light; add orange juice, sugar, Grand Marnier, and gelatin and mix until it starts to thicken. Fold in whipped cream. Pour into 7-inch soufflé dish with wax-paper collar. Freeze at least 4 hours (the soufflé will keep for a couple of weeks in freezer). Remove from freezer a half-hour before serving. Remove collar. Roll edge in ground praline.

Praline:

½ cup sugar	½ cup slivered toasted almonds
2 tablespoons water	

Boil sugar and water in heavy-bottomed saucepan until caramelized. Stir in almonds and pour on greased baking sheet. When cold and crisp, grind or pound into crumbs. This will keep indefinitely in tightly closed jar in refrigerator.

❧

F / R2
GRASSHOPPER MOLD
12 servings

2 envelopes unflavored gelatin	½ cup crème de menthe
1 cup cold water	½ cup white crème de cacao
1 cup sugar	2 cups heavy cream, whipped
¼ teaspoon salt	Garnish: whipped cream,
6 eggs, separated	chocolate shavings, optional

In medium saucepan sprinkle gelatin over water. Add ½ cup of the sugar, salt, and egg yolks; stir until thoroughly blended. Place over low heat; stir constantly until gelatin dissolves and mixture thickens slightly, about 5 minutes. Remove from heat; stir in crème de menthe and crème de cacao. Chill, stirring occasionally, until mixture mounds slightly when dropped from spoon.

Beat egg whites in large bowl until stiff but not dry. Gradually add remaining ½ cup sugar and beat until very stiff. Fold whites into gelatin mixture. Then fold in whipped cream. Turn into 12-cup mold. Chill until firm. If desired, garnish with additional whipped cream and chocolate shavings.

❧

F
SPOOM
6 servings

1 cup sugar	1 quart lemon sherbet or ice,
½ cup water	softened
4 egg whites	Dry red or rosé wine, or
	champagne
	6 large strawberries, optional

Combine sugar and water and cook over high heat until mixture reaches 238 degrees on a candy thermometer (soft-ball stage *). Beat the whites until very stiff. While syrup is still hot, pour it in a thin thread very slowly over beaten whites, beating vigorously all the time. Combine this meringue with the sherbet in champagne or other stemmed glasses or in individual sauce dishes, filling the glass three-quarters full. Freeze. This will keep for a week or so. When ready to serve, lace each serving with wine, top with strawberry and serve immediately.

🙰

R1

STRAWBERRY BAVARIAN

6 servings

1 quart strawberries, hulled	3 tablespoons cherry-flavored
2 envelopes unflavored gelatin	liqueur
¼ cup cold water	2 cups heavy cream, whipped
½ cup sugar	Whole strawberries for garnish

Puree strawberries in blender. In a saucepan soften gelatin in cold water. Add to puree with sugar. Heat and stir until gelatin is dissolved. Cool and add cherry liqueur. Chill, stirring occasionally, until mixture begins to thicken. Fold in whipped cream and spoon into 8-cup mold or serving bowl until mixture is set. To serve, unmold and top with whole berries.

---

* Soft-ball stage can be tested as follows without a thermometer: Have a cupful of cold, not ice, water ready. Drop a little of boiling syrup into the water. When the syrup can be gathered up in the fingers into a soft ball that holds its shape until pressure is removed, it has reached the soft-ball stage, 238 degrees.

ಆ

F

STRAWBERRY SORBET, OR MOUSSE

12 servings

3 pints strawberries, hulled and cleaned
2 cups sugar

Juice of 3 lemons
Juice of 3 oranges
½ cup orange liqueur

Combine strawberries with sugar and juices in blender and blend until smooth. Add orange liqueur and pour into refrigerator ice-cube trays for freezing. Freeze until mixture is partially frozen. Transfer to a large bowl and beat until mushy. Return to trays and freeze until firm. To serve, leave in refrigerator about 45 minutes before serving.

To make this sorbet into a mousse:

After mixture is partially frozen, beat until mushy. Fold in 1 stiffly beaten egg white and ½ cup heavy cream, whipped. Follow remaining directions. Or follow directions through first freezing and make several days ahead. Freeze until firm. Two hours before serving, allow to sit at room temperature 15 to 20 minutes. Then beat in blender until mushy and continue with directions.

ಆ

STRAWBERRIES WITH KIRSCH

10 servings

2 quarts strawberries
⅔ cup confectioners' sugar, or to taste
3 tablespoons kirsch (or other suitable liqueur such as Cointreau, Grand Marnier, or orange Triple Sec)
Crème Fraîche (page 57)

Wash and hull berries; place in bowl and sprinkle with sugar, then kirsch. The quantities really depend on the sweetness and flavor of the strawberries. Chill in the refrigerator for a maximum of 2 hours or the berries become too soft.

The strawberries are most attractive when served from a large glass bowl or in footed goblets. Pass Crème Fraîche separately.

☙

F / R3

KATE'S LEMON SQUARES

Makes approximately 100

Crust:

1 cup butter, softened	2 cups unbleached flour
½ cup confectioners' sugar	Pinch of salt

Topping:

4 eggs	6 tablespoons fresh lemon juice
2 cups granulated sugar	6 tablespoons lemon rind
6 tablespoons flour	Confectioners' sugar for topping

For crust: Combine ingredients; blend with fingers or pastry blender, then pat evenly into 10-x-15-inch jelly-roll pan. Bake at 350 degrees for 20 minutes.

Meanwhile, beat eggs slightly; stir in sugar, flour, lemon juice and rind. Mix well and spread over baked crust. Bake for 25 minutes more. When cooled, cut into squares; remove and sift with confectioners' sugar.

To freeze: bake, cut into squares and freeze. To serve, defrost and sprinkle with confectioners' sugar.

❧

LEMON ICE WITH WINE

6 servings

6 generous scoops lemon ice or
lemon sherbet
½ cup white wine

2½ to 3 tablespoons orange
liqueur

Spoon the sherbet into individual serving dishes, preferably glass stemware. Combine the wine and orange liqueur and pour over the ice just before serving.

❧

F / R2

ERNA'S LACE COOKIES

Makes approximately 30

⅔ cup blanched almonds
½ cup butter
Dash salt

½ cup sugar
1 tablespoon unbleached flour
2 tablespoons milk

Grind almonds. Melt butter in skillet. Add salt, sugar and flour and stir over low heat until sugar melts. Add almonds and milk and blend well, stirring until mixture thickens a little. Cool about 1 minute. Drop from a teaspoon on greased and floured cookie sheets. Leave room between them because they spread. You can get about 10 cookies per regular sheet. Bake at 350 degrees for 6 to 8 minutes, or until golden-brown. Cool only long enough for cookies to firm up so they can be removed from cookie sheet with a knife. If they set too hard return to oven briefly to soften.

These cookies can be frozen if well wrapped, or they will keep a couple of days if stored in tightly covered container and kept dry.

F / R1

DOUBLE CHOCOLATE THREAT

12 servings

For chocaholics, this is nirvana!

Brownie Crust:

⅓ cup butter
2 squares unsweetened
   chocolate
1 cup sugar
2 eggs, well beaten
⅔ cup unbleached flour

½ teaspoon baking powder
¼ teaspoon salt
1 teaspoon vanilla
½ pint heavy cream, whipped,
   for garnish

Melt butter and chocolate over low heat or in top of double boiler over hot water. Remove from heat, add sugar and eggs and mix well. Sift together flour, baking powder and salt. Stir into chocolate mixture. Add vanilla and pour into greased and floured 8- or 9-inch-square baking pan. Bake at 350 degrees for 30 to 35 minutes, until brownies are baked but not dry. Cool. Remove from pan and cut into strips wide enough to come most of the way up the sides of a 2-quart soufflé dish or charlotte mold. Cut the strips through the center to make 2 thinner layers. Line bottom and sides of dish with brownie layers. Don't worry about piecing; it won't show.

While brownies are baking, make . . .

Filling:

1½ pounds semisweet chocolate
½ cup strong coffee
3 eggs, separated

½ cup coffee liqueur
½ cup heavy cream

Melt chocolate with coffee over low heat or in top of double boiler over hot water. Remove from heat. Beat yolks until pale in color; stir into chocolate. Stir in coffee liqueur. Cool. Beat whites until stiff but not dry. Whip cream stiff. Fold whites and cream into chocolate mixture and spoon into brownie-lined dish.

Chill overnight in refrigerator, well wrapped, or freeze. To serve, defrost if frozen. To remove from pan, loosen from sides with knife, then dip into hot water to loosen and turn out onto serving plate.

Whip ½ pint heavy cream until stiff and cover top and parts of sides with cream. Serve small slices.

❧

R7

SYLVIA'S FRUITCAKE

6 pounds

Sylvia Schur's fruitcake is like no other. It has little candied fruit, lots of dried fruit in large pieces, and lots of large pieces of nuts. There is very little cake in relation to the fruit. Don't chop nuts or cut up fruit.

½ pound shelled Brazil nuts
½ pound shelled walnuts
½ pound shelled pecans
1 pound pitted dates
1 pound dried apricots
3 ounces pitted prunes, halved
1 cup diced glacéed fruit, or ½ cup diced glacéed fruit and ½ cup raisins

1 cup drained uncolored maraschino cherries
1½ cups unbleached flour
1 teaspoon baking powder
1 teaspoon salt
6 eggs
1 cup sugar
2 teaspoons vanilla
Nuts for garnish
¾ cup brandy

Line a 6-cup round cake or soufflé dish with brown paper.

Combine fruits and nuts in large bowl. Sift flour and baking powder over fruits and nuts, and combine until everything is well coated. Beat salt, eggs, sugar and vanilla until foamy. Pour egg mixture over fruits and nuts and combine thoroughly but gently. Fill prepared pan to the top with batter. Press cake mixture down in pan so it will hold shape after baking. Stud cake with additional nuts. Bake at 300 degrees for 1¼ hours, or until cake tester comes out clean. Spoon half of brandy over cake as it comes from oven. When cake cools, pour rest of brandy over it.

To store, after cake cools, wrap in cheesecloth which has been soaked in brandy. Overwrap tightly with heavy-duty aluminum foil or store in airtight container. When cheesecloth dries out, resoak in brandy.

INDEX

INDEX

cream sauce for, 43
fresh, marinade for, 180
highly processed, 12
See also names of vegetables
Verdon, René, 118
Vermicelli, 164-165
Victorian stuffed turkey, 106-107
Vinaigrette dressing, 45-46
for hot asparagus, 171
Vinegar and oil dressing, 188
Vitamins, 18
Vivarois (restaurant), 72-73
Volume-versus-weight game, 26

Wachtmeister, Ulla, 66
Waffles, 54
biscuit mix for, 53
Walnut(s)
bourbon pâté, 80
Chinese chicken and, 100-101
cucumber salad with, 179
sweet potatoes and, 172
zucchini with, 174
zucchini bread, 202-203
Warm Springs Indian fried bread, 201
Washington Post, The, 30
Waxed products, 22
Wheat flour, 24
White bean and tuna salad, 186

White sauce, 155
White wine, 33
broccoli with, 161
lemon ice with, 222
Whole-wheat bread, 24
banana, 202
Whole-wheat flour, 24, 32
Winter, Ruth, 17
Winter salad, 187
WRC-TV, 13, 30

Yellow Number 5, 20
Yogurt
additives in, 23
dressing, 185, 189
frozen, 58
thickening agents used in, 19

Zabaglione sauce, 213
Zucchini
boats, 131
kolokithopita, 145
salad, 187-188
piquant, 182
Sherley's vichy-squash, 88
stuffed, 171-172
tomato casserole, 173
walnut bread, 202-203
with walnuts, 174

ABOUT THE AUTHOR . . .

MARIAN BURROS is the well-known food editor of *The Washington Post*. As a reporter, she has taken special interest in consumer problems for a long time and broadcasts consumer features for NBC-TV. She is the author of a number of successful cookbooks, the mother of two children, and lives with her husband in Bethesda, Maryland.